Mathematics and Science for a Change

How to Design, Implement, and Sustain High-Quality Professional Development

Iris R. Weiss
Joan D. Pasley

HEINEMANN
Portsmouth, NH

Heinemann
361 Hanover Street
Portsmouth, NH 03801–3912
www.heinemann.com

Offices and agents throughout the world

Library of Congress Cataloging-in-Publication Data
Weiss, Iris R.
   Mathematics and science for a change : how to design, implement, and sustain high-quality professional development / Iris R. Weiss and Joan D. Pasley.
         p. cm.
   Includes bibliographical references.
   ISBN-13: 978-0-325-02618-3
   ISBN-10: 0-325-02618-1
   1. Mathematics teachers—In-service training. 2. Science teachers—In-service training. 3. Technology—In-service training. 4. Educational leadership.   I. Pasley, Joan Deters.   II. Title.
   QA10.5.W45 2009
   507.1—dc22   2008051166

Editor: Victoria Merecki
Production service: Matrix Productions Inc.
Production supervisor: Patricia Adams
Typesetter: Aptara, Inc.
Cover design: Bernadette Skok
Manufacturing: Valerie Cooper

Printed in the United States of America on acid-free paper
13 12 11 10 09   VP   1 2 3 4 5

Contents

Foreword

*A*s educators, we believe in the power of learning to transform ideas and practices, whether in the classroom for the students we teach and support or in professional development settings for the adult learners we are and aspire to be. This book offers guidance in improving professional development, so that the greatest learning is possible for the adult learners committed to promoting student development.

The experiences of a large number of National Science Foundation–funded Local Systemic Change (LSC) projects—across the country and over a ten-year period—have yielded many powerful lessons about quality professional development. They are offered, here, as advice from one community of practitioners to colleagues in schools, districts, universities, and non-profit organizations around the country. When educators gather at conferences, network online, or meet in study groups, they turn to one another to benefit from practice honed over time and across different settings. In this volume, the collective wisdom, that has grown out of the LSC community's experience with professional development is synthesized and made available for others to consider and apply.

If you are a practitioner wanting to improve the quality of professional development, whether you are a district mathematics or science supervisor responsible for district-wide professional development, a principal who wants to promote richer learning among staff, or a teacher leader who is seeking guidance in working with groups of classroom teachers, you will find helpful advice in this book.

The power of this volume is in its identification and presentation of a variety of insights about professional development; its organization of insights related to preparing for change, designing professional development, focusing on professional development providers, and addressing system-wide supports for sustainability; and its illustrations of those insights with examples.

Think of these insights as framing a series of questions to ask yourself as you reflect on, assess, and plan for professional development:

- **How do we . . . ?** How do we, for example, collect data on progress to improve program quality? How can we ensure quality control among multiple professional development providers? How can we assess improvements in classroom practice?

- **How important is it that . . . ?** How important is it, for example, that we develop a shared vision for professional development among administrators and teachers? Why should we articulate a common vision—and how do we do so?

- **What is the benefit of . . . ?** What is the benefit, for example, of providing coaching and mentoring services for individualized teacher support? What are the intended outcomes for the work of coaches and how do we achieve those outcomes?

The utility of this volume is in how it helps you frame important questions to pose about quality professional development, as well as find the answers to those questions. Quality professional development, though, is more than the sum total of the many good insights found in this volume. Quality professional development results from a smart and strategic plan that is implemented successfully. To that end, this volume will help you make decisions about what to focus on in your professional development program. It will offer guidance in identifying the important issues worthy of your attention and in determining which you want to focus on now, and which later. And it will prepare you to consider some of the trade-offs that you will inevitably have to make as you proceed. In short, by taking advantage of what this volume offers, you will be in a better position to make well-informed decisions, because you will be familiar with the full sweep of what constitutes quality professional development for mathematics and science teachers.

Barbara Miller

Preface

The National Science Foundation (NSF) has supported efforts to strengthen mathematics and science education since it was created more than fifty years ago. Various programs have focused on research on teaching and learning, the development of instructional materials, the preparation of new teachers, and professional development of current classroom teachers.

In 1994, NSF launched the Local Systemic Change (LSC) initiative as part of its Teacher Enhancement program. As Section Head, Promoting Standards K–8, I had the responsibility of coordinating the development of the program and refining it over time based on the lessons learned. I also had the privilege of interacting with other NSF program officers and with the community of educators who were committed to improving mathematics and science education on such a large scale.

The primary goal of the LSC initiative was to improve classroom instruction by enhancing the knowledge and skills of a large number of teachers of mathematics and science. We realized that broadening the pool of potential scientists and mathematicians and producing a science-literate citizenry required instructional improvement efforts that began at the earliest levels. We were also committed to reaching all students, including those in small rural districts and large urban districts, not just those in the suburban districts that traditionally responded to NSF funding opportunities.

The LSC initiative spanned ten years. LSC projects ranged widely—in geographical distribution, in numbers of teachers targeted, in urbanicity, in the race/ethnicity of teacher and student populations, in local resources available for teaching and learning, and in the planned interventions.

The program solicitation intentionally linked professional development with the implementation of research-based instructional materials selected by the districts, to help teachers become conversant with the materials that they would subsequently use in the classroom with their students. By involving large numbers of teachers within a district, we hoped to create a paradigm shift among a critical mass of teachers.

Projects were free to design whatever approaches they believed would be effective in their contexts, as long as they included the required elements of intensive, content-based professional development for all teachers, centered on research-based instructional materials. The expectation was that each teacher would both participate in a substantial amount of "formal" professional development and receive school-based follow-up support. A total of eighty-eight projects received LSC funding, typically for a period of five years each. By 2005, the LSC initiative had reached seventy thousand elementary- and secondary-level teachers and two million students in four thousand schools throughout the United States.

To evaluate the overall program, NSF funded a "core" evaluation focusing on the quality of the professional development, the effects of the program on teachers and their teaching, and the extent to which district policies and practices were becoming aligned with the vision underlying the LSC efforts. Local project evaluators collected data using common instruments, including classroom observation protocols, so that the results could be aggregated across projects at the national level. The fact that trained observers were going into classrooms to see whether—and if so, how—the professional development was being translated into instruction provided important formative feedback for the projects as well as for NSF.

The evaluation results indicate that the LSC efforts made a difference—in teachers, in their teaching, and in the participating education systems. Projects increased teachers' use of research-based instructional materials and enhanced the quality of classroom instruction. Participating teachers presented a higher quality of content to their students; were more likely to use investigative strategies, questioning, and sense-making practices; and more often created a classroom culture based on intellectual rigor and student engagement. Projects also built support for these instructional changes among key stakeholders and created policies and mechanisms that would help ensure continued improvement.

The efforts to involve all mathematics and science teachers resulted in having a far greater proportion of a district's teachers participate in high-quality professional development than had ever been the case when participation was entirely voluntary. Still, projects rarely came anywhere close to involving all of the teachers they had targeted, and system-wide improvement of mathematics and science instruction remained less than had been hoped.

Periodically, projects were brought together to focus on lessons learned about the design and implementation of system-wide improvement efforts. Initially the focus was on learning from one another about anticipating and overcoming challenges. Over time, the emphasis shifted to sharing lessons with the broader field. Given the opportunity, what would LSC educators tell the mathematics and science education communities about designing professional development? About preparing professional development providers? About supporting implementation of instructional materials? About engaging administrators? About sustaining reform?

Clearly, a great deal was learned in these efforts that would be helpful to practitioners charged with designing and supporting professional development for mathematics and science teachers. Educators from individual projects described the challenges they faced in addressing the wide range of teachers' content needs and explained what they learned about supporting teachers in ongoing and effective ways. They talked about the resistance they encountered among some teachers and described the strategies that proved effective in overcoming that resistance. In addition, they noted the critical importance of having school and district administrators on board.

This book reflects the wisdom gained through the LSC initiative and the hope that it will help those who plan such efforts in the future.

Susan Snyder

Acknowledgments

*T*his document is based on work supported by the National Science Foundation under Contract No. REC-9912485. This book was written by Iris R. Weiss and Joan D. Pasley of Horizon Research, Inc., with contributions from Patty Kannapel and Marianne Smith, consulting education writers.

Our sincere thanks go to the Principal Investigators and Evaluators of the Local Systemic Change projects for their willingness to share their stories and provide feedback on draft versions of this document.

Any opinions, findings, and conclusions or recommendations expressed in this material are those of the authors and do not necessarily reflect the views of the National Science Foundation.

Introduction

Structure and Content of this Guide

This guide is for school district mathematics and science supervisors and other district and school leaders who are trying to create mathematics and science classrooms that provide high-quality, engaging instruction for all students.

Part One focuses on the initial work involved in preparing for change. The first step is for program leaders to establish a vision of high-quality mathematics and science instruction that is consistent with national standards and with the ultimate goal of ensuring that *all* students have access to effective instruction in these content areas. Once the vision is established, it will be necessary to identify needs in the district, relative to realizing the vision, which will inform development of a comprehensive plan. Because teachers will be the primary change agents, the plan must focus on how to develop teachers professionally to take on the challenge of helping students meet high-level mathematics and science education standards. Program leaders must always keep in mind that the ultimate goal is to improve student learning.

Part Two discusses the design of professional development. Professional development must be designed to meet the particular needs of the district and its teachers. Some aspects of this professional development will probably take the form of intensive workshop or institute experiences to deepen teacher content knowledge and provide exemplars of, and experience with, effective instructional practices. Other experiences—particularly as the initiative moves forward—will be school-based, job-embedded activities designed both to support actual implementation and to help teachers learn to monitor student learning and adjust their instruction accordingly. Quality assurance measures should be implemented throughout, from professional development to classroom instruction to engaging teachers in evaluating their preparedness and classroom practices.

Part Three addresses the important issue of identifying, preparing, and supporting the "providers" of professional development. To build this kind of quality professional development, program leaders will need to plan carefully for identifying, preparing, and supporting professional development providers. This means identifying the skills needed to deliver professional development and selecting providers accordingly—most likely by creating provider teams with a mix of backgrounds and expertise. In order to build capacity that can be sustained over the long term, preparation of provider teams should address various forms of teacher leadership, including leadership for presenting workshops, facilitating teacher meetings and study groups, and coaching and mentoring.

Part Four deals with the system itself—how to build system-wide support for the improvement effort and how to sustain the effort over time. The change effort is not solely dependent on teachers; in fact, it is unlikely to be sustained without system-wide supports. Therefore, from the beginning and throughout the improvement initiative, program leaders should have a long-range view toward building a system that can be maintained, refined, and sustained. A culture of shared responsibility for student learning should be established consistent with existing state assessments. At the same time, program leaders should ensure that measures are in place to capture the kind of learning embodied within the program vision. It is critical to enlist the support of district and school leaders, including identifying specific actions they can take to realize the program vision. Partnerships with the mathematics and science community, as well as with parents, will also contribute to a supportive system. Sustainability should be planned from the start, by connecting the improvement effort with district priorities, developing policies that support high-quality mathematics and science instruction, and developing teacher leadership to build and sustain capacity.

Each chapter offers advice and practical suggestions based on the lessons learned by LSC project leaders and participants. The square icon indicates specific examples that you may find useful as you design and launch your own improvement effort.

Key Questions

It's up to program leaders to make sure the work stays focused around a vision of high-quality mathematics and science instruction. Despite the pressures of implementation, leaders can offer guidance and sustain the vision by posing key questions:

- What do students need to learn?
- What kinds of instruction will facilitate that learning?
- What kinds of knowledge and assistance do teachers need to ensure engaging learning opportunities?
- What do various stakeholders need to do to provide this knowledge and assistance?
- How will teachers and district leaders know students are achieving learning goals?

Perspectives on Change

The advice, examples, and anecdotes in these pages provide evidence that teamwork and thoughtful planning can change the way teachers teach mathematics and science. In today's education policy arena, strengthening STEM (science, technology, engineering, and mathematics) education is a critical issue. Supporting and sustaining well-designed professional development can make a definitive difference in school districts and the communities they serve.

The program leaders whose stories are told in this guide believe that what they have learned about what it takes to help teachers implement high-quality mathematics and science instruction is definitely transferable, and that leaders elsewhere will gain from their experiences. They advise school district leaders to start by developing a vision of high-quality mathematics and science education, next to determine the funding required to realize the vision, and then to seek the resources to do so. If district leaders are willing to tackle these challenges, there is much they can learn from the lessons shared here.

THE BIG PICTURE

Vision, Goals, and Working with Teachers

Part

I

*I*n recent years, the publication of national standards in mathematics and science education has moved educators toward greater consensus about what students need to know and be able to do in these two content areas. The *Curriculum and Evaluation Standards for School Mathematics* and the *Principles and Standards for School Mathematics* published in 1989 and 2000, respectively, by the National Council of Teachers of Mathematics (NCTM) and the *National Science Education Standards* published by the National Research Council in 1996 created a vision for mathematics and science education that goes beyond memorization of facts, formulas, and vocabulary (NCTM 1989; NCTM 2000; NRC 1996).

These mathematics and science education standards call for classroom instruction that differs considerably from what many teachers learned during their preservice education—and from what they had previously been doing in their classrooms. (See Figure 1.) To move toward this new vision requires focusing intensely on assisting teachers as they change their ways of thinking and behaving in the classroom.

The first step is to lay the groundwork for the professional development that will be at the center of the improvement effort. This groundwork involves establishing a vision of high-quality mathematics and science instruction within the district; identifying needs; setting professional development goals; and giving thoughtful attention and planning to working with teachers as professionals and key change agents.

According to the NCTM, mathematics instruction should align factual knowledge and procedural proficiency with conceptual knowledge. It should involve students in reflecting on their thinking and learning from their mistakes. It should also challenge students to learn increasingly more sophisticated mathematical ideas and should prepare them to apply their knowledge of mathematics to real-life settings.

A new vision of science instruction has also been developed—one that highlights the role of inquiry in science disciplines. According to the *National Science Education Standards*, as part of their science learning, students need to make observations; pose questions; examine information sources; plan and conduct investigations; review their current knowledge in light of experimental evidence; and use tools to gather and interpret data, propose explanations, and communicate results.

For more information on the mathematics and science education standards, see www.nctm.org/standards and www.nsta.org/standards.

Figure 1

Vision and Goal Setting 1

*T*he fact that everyone wants to improve teaching and learning does not mean that everyone has the same view of high-quality mathematics and science instruction, nor that everyone has the same vision of how to go about the improvement efforts. Program leaders need to work to create a sense of "we're all in this together," not only at the beginning of any new initiative, but throughout the process.

Develop a Shared Vision with Top Administration Support

To create a successful, sustainable mathematics/science education improvement effort, programs need support from top district decision makers. This influential group has the power to establish policies and motivate school principals and teachers to dedicate their energies and resources to improving instruction in mathematics and science.

Everyone—the superintendent, members of the school board or local school council, and the leadership of teachers' unions—must be approached and educated, so that there is a shared understanding of the program vision of high-quality mathematics and science instruction. Each leader should understand what effective instruction looks like and how professional development helps classroom teachers learn to provide this kind of instruction.

EDUCATING ADMINISTRATORS

Program leaders should meet with district administrators early on to describe the vision for improvement. Explain how the program is in synch with district and state education goals, and present research supporting the effectiveness of the new approaches to mathematics and science education. Virtually all districts in the country are under pressure to improve student performance in mathematics, and increasingly in science, on state assessments. The assessments differ in each state, but many reflect the national mathematics and science education standards cited in Part One of this book. Point out these connections to superintendents and other district leaders, and build a case for the initiative, based on the premise that a new approach to mathematics and science education will be required if students are to meet the standards.

Following this "up front" work with district administrators, program leaders can contribute to regularly scheduled principal meetings or engage in one-on-one outreach to principals to promote the overall vision and goals of the initiative. Invite principals to visit classrooms and professional development events to observe program activities. Scheduling meetings to report on progress of the science or mathematics program is another approach to administrator engagement.

When key district administrators are engaged in initiatives over time, the efforts are more likely to move toward lasting change. Building a shared vision requires strategic planning, not only at the beginning of the initiative, but also as program activities and district needs evolve. (For more on this topic, see Chapter 9.)

☐ Building Administrator Support: A Team Approach

To develop a vision of inquiry-based science instruction, some initiatives have sent district leadership teams to the National Science Resources Center Elementary Science Leadership Institute in Washington, D.C. While attending the institute, teams get together and begin drafting district plans for their science education program. ■

Remember That the Ultimate Goal of Professional Development Is to Improve Student Learning

Because time and resources for professional development are limited, it is essential that program leaders target priority needs within the district. Traditionally, professional development available to mathematics and science teachers was governed by supply and demand. University faculty advertised a workshop or institute, the topic of which may or may not have been directly related to the district's curriculum, and interested teachers enrolled. It was then up to the teachers to determine how to apply in their classrooms what they learned. Such a slapdash approach to professional development is inadequate. Priorities need to be established by the district, ideally connecting teacher professional development to instructional materials.

Given budgetary and time constraints, program leaders have to make choices. It will not be possible to address in depth all of the mathematics/science content included in state and district standards documents. Identifying aspects of the curriculum that are in particular need of more work helps to narrow the focus of professional development to a more realistic plan.

☐ Analyzing Student Test Results

One science education initiative administered student items from the Trends in International Mathematics and Science Study[1] (TIMSS). Looking at test results "confirmed the need to strengthen the physical science strand of the curriculum and increase instructional emphasis on graphing and interpreting graphs." Other programs identified topics on their state tests on which the district's students had performed poorly and determined their professional development priorities based on the data collected.   ■

SUPPORT FOR TEACHERS

Meaningful professional development is targeted at teacher learning, with the ultimate goal of improving learning opportunities for students. With this in mind, leaders will ask questions like "What kind of professional development do teachers need to help students learn to reason statistically and apply this reasoning to real-life consumer situations?" rather than "What kind of professional development will persuade teachers to stop telling students 'the answers' and encourage them to explore problems in depth?" The difference in approach is clear: the ultimate goal of professional development is *not* to "fix teachers" but to help teachers provide the kinds of learning opportunities that students need to meet challenging mathematics and science education standards.

[1] See timss.bc.edu/timss2003.html

Build a Flexible Professional Development Plan

Once vision, goals, and needs are identified, program leaders should develop an overall professional development plan. Decisions need to be made about how to launch the program, in particular:

- determining costs, which may include compensation for participating schools and teachers
- introducing the professional development program to the intended audience
- identifying teachers for immediate and future participation
- articulating requirements and guidelines for participation and follow-up

PARTICIPATION OPTIONS

Some program leaders choose to involve all of the mathematics and science teachers in a district from the beginning, with the idea of providing both formal professional development and opportunities for practice over an extended period. Others start with a subset of teachers, either working one school at a time or with one or two grade levels, and expanding to other schools or grades in later years. Factors that influence these plans include student needs, teacher readiness, administrator interest and support, and available funding.

ADDRESSING TEACHERS' CONCERNS

For many teachers, concerns about classroom management and logistical issues will precede concerns about the more substantive matters of content and pedagogy. Professional development activities should be designed to accommodate these concerns, balancing workshop components that deal with immediate, basic concerns with those that focus on longer-term issues in improving quality of practice. One program leader explains,

> In our experience, basically all of the teachers have a very similar lack of knowledge of pedagogy and the content in the instructional materials initially. Teachers who have had a year of work with the kits have different levels of concern than those who are new to kit use. So as the project proceeds, the variety of professional development needs to expand.

Savvy leaders anticipate that plans will need to change. Consider whether particular aspects of the professional development program are working as intended, and examine the implications for fine-tuning the program. By making time to reflect with other key stakeholders—including professional development providers, evaluators, and participating teachers—district leaders learn how to continuously improve their efforts. Leaders should be prepared to adapt to evolving district needs as well as to concerns of participating teachers. This does not mean jumping on every new element that pops up. To remain on course, the overall plan should follow a planned trajectory, but it should also allow for flexibility to address needs that arise.

☐ Examples of Refining Professional Development Efforts Over Time

- One K–8 mathematics and science program offered Structured-Use Workshops to address the content in district instructional materials. After teachers attended the workshops, they could choose from an initial menu of professional development offerings. As the program progressed, the workshops were reviewed and refined, and a second tier of workshops was created to help teachers deepen their content knowledge, reflect on and improve their classroom practice, and build teacher leadership skills.

- A K–8 science program developed an initial design that revolved around science summer institutes. In order to engage teachers who otherwise might not participate, principals requested professional development opportunities during the school year, and program staff modified the summer institute design accordingly. When new state science standards were released, program leaders reworked the summer institute's agenda to familiarize teachers with the new standards. They also analyzed the new standards and described how they aligned with concepts in the science kits that teachers were using in the classroom.

- When science program leaders realized that their initial professional development design was not leading to effective use of the student instructional materials, they revised the plan. For each science module, a storyline was used to orient teachers to how various activities helped students learn targeted science concepts. During both initial professional development and "booster" sessions, teachers had time to consider the storyline of the instructional materials in light of science learning goals.

- "Kit Clubs" were used by a science initiative to introduce teachers to science modules. Program leaders noticed that the focus on kits resulted in a "mechanical" approach to teaching science, because many teachers treated units as a series of disjointed activities rather than a curriculum to engage students in under-standing science. Accordingly, Kit Clubs were replaced by intro-ductory professional development in the form of a "Beginning Teachers Summer Institute." The institutes were designed to provide teachers with an initial experience with inquiry, which involved learning the science content embedded within the units and lessons within the units. Changing the emphasis of professional development to inquiry in learning about the science units equipped teachers with a model for using inquiry as a classroom teaching strategy.   ■

Professional Development

2

Setting the Stage

*I*f program leaders are to assist teachers in working toward a shared goal of improved student learning, it is critical that they approach teachers as professionals. When the goal of improved student achievement in mathematics and science is considered the highest priority, district leaders and teachers are more willing to work in concert.

It is up to program leaders to show teachers how they can build on their existing capabilities, while also acquiring new skills. The first steps to setting this professional tone include:

- making sure teachers understand what will be required of them to help students achieve the standards
- being responsive to teachers who are not convinced that change is necessary, as well as to those who are eager to change
- working to build an atmosphere of trust and respect

Build a Persuasive Case for Professional Development

An essential ingredient in building a case for professional development is to draw attention to student learning and how it can be improved, rather than emphasizing teachers' limitations.

Program leaders need to give teachers opportunities to see the potential benefit of professional development, and they should create experiences that leave room for teachers to examine weak areas of their practice in an atmosphere where it is safe for them to feel "puzzled." When a teacher is motivated to say, "I've got to find out more," program leaders are prepared to respond and fill in the knowledge gap.

Ideally, teachers will welcome the chance to work with district leaders to support student attainment of challenging mathematics and science goals. However, it would be naïve to assume that all teachers will immediately embrace new modes of mathematics and science instruction. Teachers who are comfortable with instructional approaches they have relied on throughout their careers may be particularly reluctant to accept new, unfamiliar programs.

In the words of one mathematics program leader, secondary teachers are especially difficult to engage because "they believe they know the mathematics and thus don't need any help." Other program leaders report similar experiences with teachers who either don't think they need more instruction in subject matter or pedagogy, or see no need to learn content outside their grade-level expertise. In particular, teachers who work in high-achieving districts may see little need to change their instruction.

☐ Using Introductory Sessions to Gain Teacher Support

To open up teachers to the possibility of change in mathematics teaching and learning, program leaders invited a group of secondary mathematics teachers to a "get acquainted" meeting. As this three-hour meeting began, program leaders emphasized that the decision to move forward with the initiative had not yet been made. Next, teachers were asked about their educational goals for students. A list of common goals was compiled, many of which corresponded with the NCTM standards. In the next activity, teachers assigned letter grades to their schools, according to how well their students were reaching the common list of goals. The mean grade was a C, with an assortment of B's and D's.

More questions and discussions followed, during which teachers listed obstacles to student achievement, most of which were factors external to teaching. Toward the end of the workshop, teachers responded to a set of "forced choice" questions concerning beliefs about effective instruction and curriculum. Program leaders projected the questionnaire data, to show the range of teachers' attitudes toward the program, as well as how receptive they were to inquiry-based or student-centered instruction. ■

☐ Using Analysis of Student Work to Build a Case for Professional Development

According to one program leader, activities designed to examine student work were helpful in highlighting the need for improvement in instruction:

> Once teachers begin to look at their own student work in the company of peers, specific issues related to instructional practice and learning goals begin to emerge. At this point, coursework that emphasized content and inquiry becomes meaningful and relevant. ∎

Be Responsive Not Only to Teachers Who Are Willing to Change, but Also to Those Who Are Resistant

In the initial stages of professional development, it makes sense to concentrate on teachers who are receptive to change. In this manner, districts can "work out the kinks," gain credibility, develop a base of support among faculty and administrators, and build a pool of change-minded teachers to serve as advocates, role models, and mentors to reluctant participants. One program leader put it this way: "Maybe persistence is the key, along with a critical mass of enthused participants beginning to exert some peer pressure."

Working with teachers who want to change their instructional practices does not imply excluding those who are not convinced that change is needed. Professional development leaders suggest reaching out to all teachers and actively soliciting their views. If skeptics are involved in professional development—and treated with respect and openness throughout—resistance often dissolves, as teachers try new approaches and see positive results with students. One program leader remarked, "If we can get teachers into Year Two training and implementation, they become more vested with the change and accept it." Another program leader shared a similar view: "Devise some strategy to bring in the reluctant adopters because it is through their participation that the program might be institutionalized."

☐ Addressing Resistance to Improvement Efforts

Mathematics and science education initiatives relied on a variety of strategies to understand resistance to reform and to fully inform teachers of the nature of the initiative. Strategies included:

- Interviewing a sample of teachers to determine reasons for resistance
- Preparing professional development providers for questions and challenges that teachers might pose
- Listening to resistant teachers and responding to their concerns
- Providing resistant teachers with opportunities to visit classrooms that reflected the program vision
- Assigning mentors to work one-on-one with resistant teachers
- Extending invitations to resistant teachers throughout the program   ■

☐ Recruiting Reluctant Teachers

Leaders of a K–8 science initiative, in collaboration with principals, identified resistant teachers and designed modified workshops for them around science kits central to the program. After the workshops, these teachers became more willing participants, and their involvement influenced other teachers who had been resistant. Resistant teachers targeted for these workshops often became their strongest advocates. As one teacher noted, "There is very distinct pressure from other teachers to get involved with [the improvement initiative]."   ■

Make It Convenient for Teachers to Participate in Professional Development

One aspect of treating teachers as professionals is recognizing the host of logistical barriers to participation in professional development and trying to make it as easy as possible for teachers to participate. These barriers include limited availability of substitute teachers to fill in for released teachers, along with competing family obligations after school, on weekends, or in the summer. Leaders of mathematics and science education initiatives have found that teachers are most likely to attend professional development offered during the school day. In the words of one program leader, "You have to do [professional development] during the school day. I didn't believe that when I started this project. It's the only way to get full participation."

☐ Providing Multiple Options

One program leader suggested multiple participation options for teachers:

Additional venues, such as Saturday mornings, short institutes, after-school sessions, and class visits need to be exploited to reach those teachers who for a variety of reasons will never attend a summer institute.

Other programs have implemented online courses to make professional development more accessible to teachers. If sufficient resources are available, offering stipends or course credit can also be a powerful incentive for participation.   ■

Part One: Further Readings

American Association for the Advancement of Science. 1989. Science for all Americans: A Project 2061 report on literacy goals in science, mathematics, and technology. Washington, DC: Author.

American Association for the Advancement of Science/Project 2061. 1993. *Benchmarks for science literacy.* New York: Oxford University Press.

Banilower, E., Cohen, K., Pasley, J., & Weiss, I. 2008. *Effective science instruction: What does research tell us?* Portsmouth, NH: RMC Research Corporation, Center on Instruction.

Ma, L. 1999. *Knowing and teaching elementary mathematics: Teachers' understanding of fundamental mathematics in China and the United States.* Mahwah, NJ: Erlbaum.

Michaels, S., Shouse, A. W., & Schweingruber, H. A. 2008. *Ready, set, science!: Putting research to work in K–8 science classrooms.* Board on Science Education, Center for Education, Division of Behavioral and Social Sciences and Education. Washington, DC: The National Academies Press.

National Council of Teachers of Mathematics. 1989. *Curriculum and evaluation standards for school mathematics.* Reston, VA: Author.

National Council of Teachers of Mathematics. 2000. *Principles and standards for school mathematics.* Reston, VA: Author.

National Research Council. 1996. *National science education standards.* Washington, DC: National Academy Press.

National Research Council. 2000. *Inquiry and the national science education standards.* Washington, DC: National Academy Press.

National Research Council. 2005. *How students learn: History, mathematics, and science in the classroom,* ed. M. S. Donovan & J. D. Bransford. Washington, DC: National Academy Press.

National Research Council. 2005. *How students learn: Mathematics in the classroom,* ed. M. S. Donovan & J. D. Bransford. Washington, DC: National Academy Press.

National Research Council. 2005. *How students learn: Science in the classroom,* ed. M. S. Donovan & J. D. Bransford. Washington, DC: National Academy Press.

National Research Council. 2006. *Taking science to school: Learning and teaching science in grades K–8,* ed. R. A. Duschl, H. A. Schweingruber, & A. W. Shouse. Washington, DC: National Academy Press.

Stigler, J. W., & Hiebert, J. 1999. *The teaching gap: Best ideas from the world's teachers for improving education in the classroom.* New York: Free Press.

Weiss, I. R., Pasley, J. D., Smith, P. S., Banilower, E. R., & Heck, D. J. 2003. *Looking inside the classroom: A study of K–12 mathematics and science education in the United States.* Chapel Hill, NC: Horizon Research, Inc.

DESIGNING PROFESSIONAL DEVELOPMENT

*A*s program leaders begin planning the specific professional development activities that will drive the improvement effort, there are many issues to consider. This section begins with general advice about planning, followed by chapters devoted to two types of professional development: intensive, centralized professional development; and job-embedded, school-based activities.

3 | *Strategic Design*

T here is no formula for the design of professional development that will be effective in every setting. However, there are some general principles that program leaders should keep in mind in planning efforts that fit their particular context, often including both centralized professional development strategies and job-embedded activities at individual school sites.

Tailor Professional Development to Fit the School Community's Needs and Advance Program Goals

Professional development design can include a combination of centralized, large-group activities, such as summer institutes, and more dispersed year-round, school-based support for smaller groups of teachers. What matters most is that the design fit the circumstances, so that all teachers can experience a supportive learning atmosphere. Those in charge of planning may find that they have to avoid falling into old habits and resist using a professional development model that may have been successful in the past but may not work under current conditions. Enabling innovation in schools calls for innovative thinking by program leaders, which means entertaining new ideas tailored to the unique and evolving needs of the district, the schools, and the teachers.

The changing teacher population is an ongoing challenge for professional development planners. Even in districts with relatively stable faculty, periods of high turnover and/or mobility across grades or schools may affect professional development programming. Program leaders need to plan for these contingencies—for example, by integrating introductory-level workshops with continuous, ongoing professional development experiences to accommodate the needs of new teachers in the district.

TEACHER INSTITUTES

Workshops and institutes are centralized professional development strategies that can accommodate large numbers of teachers. Typically, these venues bring teachers together from various sites to focus on a particular topic, which is presented or facilitated by an "expert." The advantages of this approach include maintaining quality control and establishing a shared experience for teachers. Summer institutes—intensive professional development extending over a period of days or weeks—provide teachers with "immersion" experiences. There is enough time to address instructional materials and elements of content in depth, as well as to create a strong support system and learning community.

On the other hand, emerging research on professional development indicates that relying on workshops and institutes alone may not be sufficient (Elmore 2002; Garet et al. 2001; Loucks-Horsley et al. 2003). Transferring teacher knowledge to the classroom is a priority that needs more work; it is difficult for large, centralized venues to provide ongoing opportunities for discussion and reflection that teachers can relate to their work with students.

JOB-EMBEDDED ACTIVITIES

There are many professional development options available to complement workshops and institutes; program leaders can choose site-based meetings during the school year, which might include grade-level discussion groups, coaching, mentoring, demonstration lessons, action research, and/or lesson study. Each activity requires special knowledge and skill to create and facilitate, and each requires careful implementation. When compatible with the needs and interests of participating teachers, these practices can be extremely effective in building on what teachers experience in centralized professional development sessions.

Programs may need to develop their "professional development repertoire" gradually over time to ensure that every session that is offered is of high quality. One approach is not inherently better than another. Some program leaders begin with centralized professional development, followed by school-based approaches to help teachers with implementation. Others have found it helpful to use both approaches simultaneously to support "veteran" teachers, as well as to help initiate teachers into the program.

Address Teachers' Diverse Backgrounds and Needs

Teachers enter professional development with varied content backgrounds and classroom experience. Some teachers have limited background in mathematics and science content and in standards-based approaches; others are relatively well versed in disciplinary content and have piloted or used "reform" programs. This reality compels professional development planners to consider how to present content accessible to all, despite differences in knowledge. Clearly, one size does not fit all.

FLEXIBLE, COHERENT DESIGN

To complicate the picture, teacher pedagogical knowledge can prove to be just as varied as their content knowledge. For some, starting with general themes of "teaching for understanding" and "assessment in the service of student learning" is appropriate. Others may be ready for a "second level" of professional development, working on the nature of inquiry, constructivism, use of student notebooks, and student learning styles. Organizing sessions using a tiered design that offers choices can be adapted to reach all participants at the optimal level.

☐ Scaffolding Professional Development

Accommodating the various levels of teacher knowledge and skill can include providing introductory-level workshops in the mix of options for continuous, ongoing professional development. For one mathematics improvement project, this meant establishing district-wide, grade-level-specific curriculum implementation sessions for teachers. To prepare teachers to use the new, standards-based instructional materials, sessions dealt with the content and flow of the new materials, one unit at a time. Over the course of the project, professional development options grew in response to teacher needs. Summer institutes continued, led by national experts on the instructional materials. New options included school-based study groups and extra coaching for teachers in high-needs schools. For the district's "high flying" teachers, a site-based master's degree program was designed and delivered by higher-education faculty.

A cautionary note: A flexible mix of sessions can inadvertently result in an incoherent "smorgasbord" of professional development offerings. To advance program goals, leaders need to build cohesive structures and logical pathways for teachers to move along, so that each set of professional experiences builds on the one before. ∎

☐ Three-Tier Model for Teachers

A K–8 science program developed a three-tier professional development program model:

Tier I: Designed for new teachers who needed to become familiar with inquiry-based teaching strategies and with implementing science kits for their grade level. Professional development was focused on kit training and inquiry and included a support and mentoring program.

Tier II: Designed for more experienced teachers, professional development concentrated on theme-based courses in the content area, followed by instructional strategies and/or study groups for each course.

Tier III: Provided leadership opportunities for teachers, including a master's program and opportunities to co-teach professional development sessions. ∎

☐ A Five-Strand Model for Various Stakeholders

In another K–8-science program, professional development was offered through five different strands, each structured to meet the needs of the participants.

1. **Nuts and Bolts:** An introduction to hands-on science materials designed for teachers new to the instructional materials

2. **Content and Pedagogy:** Ongoing professional development for experienced teachers ready to focus on content background, pedagogical content knowledge, and effective teaching strategies

3. **Leadership Development:** Opportunities for lead teachers in a position to solidify their science background while sharing their expertise at their own school sites

4. **Administrators:** Support for administrators' supervision of science teaching, and assistance in creating a vision for science instruction in their schools

5. **Science Resource Teachers:** Representative teachers from each participating district making up a master team who, together with the project director, form the grassroots core of the project   ■

Collect Data on Progress to Improve Program Quality

A plan to achieve improvement in mathematics and science education may look brilliant on paper, but if implementation is inadequate, a lot of time, energy, and resources will be squandered. From the beginning, program leaders should establish a systematic plan for collecting information on progress and problems, and they should use those data to make mid-course corrections.

QUALITY CONTROL: PROFESSIONAL DEVELOPMENT PROVIDERS

Quality control is especially important when multiple providers are delivering professional development. Program leaders should include in their design ongoing communication, consultation, observation, mentoring, and formative feedback, with and among professional development providers.

☐ An Apprenticeship Model for Professional Development Providers

Several projects implemented a model in which providers participated in a training institute and then were observed by more experienced providers as they facilitated a workshop. After the workshop, the novice trainers received feedback from the veterans before assuming their job responsibilities.   ■

ASSESSING PROGRESS: CLASSROOM OBSERVATIONS

What happens in the classrooms of participating teachers is a very important measure of the effectiveness of professional development. Program leaders should build in mechanisms to visit classrooms and talk with teachers to see how they are applying what they learned to their work with students.

☐ Classroom "Walk-Throughs"

One program included program leaders, support staff, principals, and curriculum coordinators in classroom walk-throughs as a way to take a snapshot of what was happening in classrooms. These kinds of observations can pinpoint strengths and weaknesses in teacher implementation, and program leaders can apply feedback to address weaknesses in ongoing professional development.　■

☐ Room for Improvement

The leader of a secondary mathematics program shared results of classroom visits to observe teachers who had participated in professional development centered on mathematically rich student tasks. According to the observer, instruction did not always reflect the goals of professional development:

> The teacher had written the questions on the board and students came up to the board and filled in the answers. In going over the questions, the teacher played a major role in this lesson, talking most of the time while trying to get students to answer his questions using the fill-in-the-blank format that he had set up on the board. The questioning was task-oriented in arriving at a product or result, but lacked purpose aimed at developing students' conceptual understanding.

In a similar case, the leader of an elementary science program noted that aspects of the professional development, such as graphic organizers and use of predictions, were incorporated into lessons, but there was clearly "room for improvement in every classroom." These observations signaled the program leader to devote more attention to questioning strategies and lesson closure in subsequent professional development sessions.[2]　■

CRITICAL FRIENDS

Allowing teachers to act as "critical friends" in monitoring one another's practice can be helpful in program evaluation and improvement. Critical friends meetings can be effective in bringing about mid-course corrections, because teachers will see for themselves where they need to develop additional knowledge and skills. During these gatherings, teachers share and discuss student work, identifying

[2]See detailed descriptions of observed lessons and insights from program leaders at www.horizon-research.com/LSC/news/pasley2002.php

problems in their own implementation, as well as needs for future professional development.[3]

PARTICIPANT INTERVIEWS

Interviewing teachers who participate in training institutes may also serve as a useful feedback mechanism to gauge the quality of professional development and the needs of professional development providers. Initiatives collected feedback via end-of-workshop evaluations from participants, as well as by surveying participants periodically over the course of the project. Conversations with teachers can also yield information on what teachers believe was most helpful and what, if anything, they think was missing from professional development, now that they have begun implementing the program.

[3]See the description of the "critical friends" process at the National School Reform Faculty website: www.nsrfharmony.org

Workshops and Institutes | 4

Designing Intensive Professional Development

*E*fforts to improve mathematics and science teaching and learning often include some centralized professional development, where teachers are brought together for workshops or institutes. This chapter highlights some important elements for program leaders to address in designing workshops and institutes for mathematics and science teachers.

Build a Collegial Atmosphere of Trust, Mutual Respect, and Openness to Ideas

Hallmarks of quality professional development are evident in settings where teachers feel comfortable sharing ideas, admitting their weaknesses, collaborating with facilitators and peers, and openly reflecting on issues related to teaching and learning. This kind of model contrasts markedly with traditional professional development activities, which are often one-time-only events featuring "top-down" communication.

An observer attending a science education workshop found that the positive atmosphere enhanced the work of teachers: "The relationship among participants was congenial, collaborative, and professional; the discussions seemed open, candid, and reflective." Another observer remarked, "All the

professional development offerings reflected the expectation that beliefs and assumptions need to be brought to light and discussed, and
that all participating teachers have much to share and give in the way
of dialogue and collaboration."

Professional development activities can be structured in ways
that promote dialogue and a joint sense of purpose, so that all participants are encouraged to contribute. Small-group discussion, collaborative problem solving, discussions of student work, and personal
reflections on classroom experiences are particularly conducive to
promoting an "open" atmosphere of trust and respect.

☐ Collaborative Culture

One teacher expressed appreciation for the collaborative experience as
follows:

> I was with other teachers, hearing about what they had done, in-
> stead of just figuring out what to do on my own all the time.

Said another:

> An aspect [of the workshop] that made a great impression on me
> is the interaction and sharing that took place. Our profession is
> designed where we go into our rooms, do our job, and have very
> little opportunity to share ideas and methods with other educators
> in the same grade.   ■

☐ Portrait of Successful Inquiry and Collaboration

Evaluators noted the effectiveness of a K–8 mathematics and science
improvement program in developing a culture of inquiry, dialogue, and
collaboration:

> At the core of the program there was a deep belief in inquiry,
> constructivist learning, and reflection on classroom practice.
> Beyond that, [program leaders] believed in the inherent value of
> a model in which teachers instruct other teachers in things they
> know well. These values permeated the majority of the activities,
> as well as the communications and general ambience of [the pro-
> gram]. Program leaders made a great effort to share these values
> with all participants in the program. We never saw consultants,
> scientists or teacher leaders . . . treat participants without respect,
> or discount their contributions. Dialogue and collaboration was a
> key design principle, built into every aspect of professional devel-
> opment.   ■

☐ Enabling Risk Taking

A strong culture of collaboration and mutual respect characterized each professional development session provided by a K–8 mathematics initiative. Teachers in these sessions listened to one other, shared ideas and experiences, and reflected on their practice as mathematics educators. While facilitating discussions, session leaders gave examples from their own classroom experiences. As they spoke with peers, teachers often took intellectual risks and were willing to reveal major deficiencies in their own mathematical understanding. Built-in time for reflection was another plus for teachers.   ■

☐ Time to Reflect

During a summer institute, teachers were asked to reflect on specific questions, write their responses in their journals, and participate in a facilitated discussion of those reflections. All perspectives and comments were valued in what became a highly collegial learning environment. This collaborative, seminar-like atmosphere can be duplicated in large groups through breakout sessions comprising diverse participant groups, such as teachers of different grade levels, teachers and administrators, or teachers and parents.   ■

Connect Professional Development to the Classroom

Teachers are concerned about their classroom responsibilities; they have little patience for activities that seem disconnected from their role as teachers. Program leaders can promote buy-in by:

- Demonstrating how professional development is linked to state standards and assessments
- Focusing on instructional materials the teachers will use in their classrooms
- Connecting professional development to student work and learning

Considering Accountability

Given the current emphasis on "accountability," it helps if teachers recognize that their own understanding of content will enable them to help students learn mathematics and science and perform well on high-stakes tests. One way to build "bridges" between professional development and classroom instruction is to focus on how to develop student mastery of state and local standards. A professional development leader remarked that "Aligning the exemplary instructional materials with the [state] mathematics standards has become an effective tool in motivating even previously lukewarm teachers and administrators." Similarly, leaders of science projects found it useful to offer professional development that linked science with mathematics and language arts, content areas that carried more weight on state assessments.

Connecting to Instructional Materials

A focus on student instructional materials helps make professional development relevant to teachers. This process may occur naturally if the mathematics or science improvement project is built around specific instructional materials. As one program leader noted, "Because the [professional development] bore a direct relationship to the texts that [teachers] would be using in the upcoming school year, teachers saw the immediate utility of the professional development."

Focusing on Student Work

Using student work as the basis for discussions can prove particularly useful to teachers. Although this kind of professional development may occur more frequently in school-based activities (discussed in Chapter 5), there may also be opportunities to feature student work in more centralized venues. To give teachers a chance to work with instructional materials under classroom-like conditions, some projects included students as well as teachers in summer workshops. Others provided samples of student work to give teachers practice in figuring out what particular students did and did not understand.

☐ Observing Student Problem Solving

A mathematics project noted that bringing a small group of students into professional development sessions was a powerful strategy. Teachers watched as students worked together to solve a problem and presented their solutions. This strategy enabled teachers to focus on students' mathematical thinking. Teachers found the activity meaningful because it involved children they recognized—as opposed to student "actors" portrayed in commercial classroom videos.   ■

Explaining the Benefits of Professional Development

Program leaders recommend translating professional development activities into practical terms that make sense to teachers. During one session focused on chemistry, teachers misunderstood the intent of a content specialist's presentation on concepts of solutions, mixtures, and suspensions that went beyond the ideas in the student module. The program leader expected more advanced content to help teachers see what came next for their students and to illustrate how the module activities served as building blocks for deeper understanding of larger concepts. To the teachers, however, the activity seemed an unnecessary digression. Explicit framing of the activity beforehand, with discussion afterward, might have enabled teachers to see the relevance of more advanced content.

□ Linking Science and Writing

In an effort to motivate reluctant teachers to attend professional development, a science improvement project created a professional development activity entitled "Good Science, Good Writing." The program leader explained:

> We offered this for one week of our summer workshops, and the title was indeed attractive to teachers, who are now under much pressure to prepare students for the writing sample on the high-stakes state test. . . . [We] didn't compromise at all what we did in terms of inquiry science. We just made very clear to the uninitiated how this science writing relates to the [state assessment] rubrics, as well as to the state science standards and the state writing standards . . . We think that we won converts by this approach. ∎

Balance Emphasis on Content, Pedagogy, and Instructional Materials

Experienced mathematics and science education leaders have found that to improve student achievement, teachers need to grow in three main areas—content knowledge, pedagogical skills, and use of high-quality instructional materials.

Striking the right balance among those areas means taking into account the value of each professional development component. Initiatives need to be conceptualized and implemented as an overall program of work, not as a "laundry list" of offerings. As one program leader commented, "It's not like Monday is content day, and Tuesday is pedagogy. You tell teachers what you're doing, and you're intentional, and you use curriculum materials to convey the content."

Introductory workshops that cover the "basics" are an efficient and important part of the overall professional development plan. But an overemphasis on exploring basic activities in the instructional materials may limit teachers' awareness of the "big picture" (how the specific activities fit into a conceptual framework, for example) and preclude deeper reflection on specific pedagogical strategies.

☐ Finding the Right Balance

Initially, a professional development model apportioned the same number of hours to each area, spending one-third of the time on content, one-third on pedagogy, and one-third on leadership development. In the original design, these three dimensions were completely separate, resulting in a "huge tension between content and pedagogy." As the initiative progressed, leaders made sure that content and pedagogy were well integrated, with content experts and teacher leaders working collaboratively to ensure that all bases were covered.

A 6–12 science program struck a balance among content, pedagogy, and instructional materials through guided "tours" of the core science units. University scientists and "unit- experienced" classroom teachers worked together to emphasize the following elements:

- Developing teachers' understanding of underlying concepts needed to teach the unit
- Translating the core unit learning targets and suggested instructional activities into a coherent, sequenced instructional plan
- Seeking input on activity design and instructional approaches based on practitioner expertise
- Demonstrating the use of equipment and technical procedures involved in more "complex" lab investigation   ■

Use Instructional Materials as a Springboard for Professional Development, but Keep the Focus on Learning Goals Rather Than Activities

Teachers' classroom practice is heavily influenced by mathematics and science instructional materials adopted in their districts (Weiss et al. 2003). Leaders of mathematics and science education programs find that content and pedagogy are more relevant and accessible to teachers when they are considered in the context of the specific instructional materials that the teachers will be using.

Teachers appreciate having opportunities to work through the instructional materials prior to using them in their classrooms; such activities help teachers develop confidence in using new texts. Introductory workshops usually focus on familiarizing teachers with the materials by having them "experience" the activities as students might, working through problems in small groups with guided discussions facilitated by core program staff, teacher leaders, or content experts.

With respect to using student instructional materials as the centerpiece of professional development, there are pitfalls to be avoided. It is important that teachers identify the key learning goals in student instructional materials and understand how each activity is intended to build on what students learned previously. Otherwise, leaders of mathematics and science initiatives find that participating teachers work with their students on activities without engaging them in the necessary "sense-making." The director of a K–8 science initiative reported that program staff felt a need to constantly remind teachers that "it's not just about kits." Professional development programs must ensure that teachers move beyond simply "doing" the student activities themselves, to learning how to use the instructional materials to promote student learning.

☐ Examining Mathematics Materials

Teachers in a K–8 mathematics program were offered Saturday workshops to examine the content and pedagogy of new elementary mathematics instructional materials adopted by the district. These workshops were not simply a time to review lists of objectives for an upcoming quarter and receive a collection of sample activities. First, knowledgeable colleagues answered questions about mathematics content and clarified the meaning of mathematical ideas that might emerge in classrooms. Second, the workshops helped teachers understand the flow and coherence of the adopted elementary mathematics instructional materials. Finally, the workshops helped teachers understand how the instructional materials could serve as a resource and what kinds of decisions they, the teachers, would have to make when using these resources. Teachers were challenged to think about how the mathematics objectives fit together and linked with or advanced prior student understandings. Simultaneously, teachers considered implications of the admittedly high mathematics standards for their students, sharing instructional ideas as they worked through the materials. The intent was to advance the basis of teachers' instructional decisions so the teachers could help their students build a logical and meaningful interpretation of the mathematics content being presented.

A 6–12 mathematics program worked with middle school mathematics teachers in multiple districts that had adopted one of three mathematics curricula: *Connected Mathematics Project*, *MathScape*, and *Seeing Mathematics in Context*. Summer institutes for teachers were organized so that mornings were devoted to working on broad mathematics topics, such as number concepts, algebraic reasoning, geometry and measurement, and data analysis, statistics, and probability. In the afternoon, teachers from schools using the same instructional materials had time to study those materials in more depth. Each curriculum group worked through activities and considered how the highlighted strand was developed in the materials.   ■

☐ Focus on Science Storylines

Key conceptual understandings formed the basis for a K–8 science program's professional development. Conceptual storylines were developed for eighteen kit-based units. The storylines were designed to help teachers see how each lesson contributed to the "big picture" of the kit and how subconcepts within a particular kit led to the development of larger concepts. In addition to storylines, program leaders developed "focus questions" for each kit to help students clarify their thinking about lesson content.

Another K–8 science program also relied heavily on conceptual storylines to guide the professional development sessions. Storylines served as prompts for teacher engagement in activities, catalysts to stimulate discussion of the student learning opportunities embedded within each lesson, and reflection on ways to teach the lessons in classrooms. Throughout the professional development sessions, the facilitator asked teachers to reflect on what they had learned during an activity and to talk about what student learning could result from the activity. To maintain a focus on the "big picture," facilitators led teachers in discussions of how each lesson built on the concepts in the previous lessons.   ■

Model and Explain Quality Instructional Practices

The adage "Teachers teach as they were taught" provides a good cautionary note. Program leaders should select providers who are able to demonstrate appropriate practices and should ensure that professional development design and implementation include modeling of effective pedagogy. By observing exemplary teaching, teachers have the opportunity to use instructional materials "richly" rather than "rotely."

If an initiative is organized around specific instructional materials, professional development should model appropriate pedagogy with those materials in mind. In this manner, teachers can develop a concrete sense of what it is like for students to experience instruction with the new materials. With materials as the centerpiece of professional development, providers should model "best practices" for engaging and motivating learners. They can focus, for example, on using questioning and discussion to deepen thinking, facilitate small-group work, or demonstrate what a rigorous but "risk-free" culture in a classroom setting might be like.

EXPLAINING HOW, WHAT, AND WHY

Modeling appropriate pedagogy is necessary, but it is only part of the task. Professional development must move beyond modeling to engage participants in detailed discussions of what they are doing and why. The objective is to create an experience in which teachers engage as learners of mathematics/science content and also step outside the "learner role" to consider pedagogical implications for their students. To communicate clearly, professional development providers need to identify the strategies they are using, explain why they are asking specific questions to monitor learner understanding, suggest classroom applications of content and pedagogy, and discuss how and why these strategies work.

Evidence from prior mathematics and science education initiatives shows that modeling of appropriate pedagogy—accompanied by explicit discussion of how and why this pedagogy helps students learn the concepts—often changes teacher beliefs about effective mathematics and science instruction. Witness the following remarks:

> I had planned to teach in the way I was taught: mostly lecture and some hands-on activities. This forum has made me see that in order for children to truly understand the concepts of science, you must let them discover. (science teacher)

> The concept development workshops taught us to listen more attentively to the children and start from there. I have a plan in my head now. This is where we're going. I need to remember to listen to what the children are saying. (science teacher)

> I look at students' work completely differently now. It opened my eyes to how many different ways there are to come to the same answer. I always wanted to bring the creative investigative kind of mathematics into my classroom, but I didn't know how to assess it.

There wasn't a smooth flow of instruction and assessment before this program. (mathematics teacher)

It has opened people's eyes up. They have brought in a lot of videos showing younger children using mathematics, which showed we have overlooked some intuitive things that kids understand. It showed that we have been in a real hurry to replace it with our own kind of thinking, instead of letting them kind of develop. I have learned to keep quiet with the kids, if they are thinking through, rather than telling them, "Well I think you ought to do it this way." (mathematics teacher)

☐ Science Study

In a professional development session on floating and sinking, science teachers worked to understand the instructional materials as though they were students. When given opportunities to reflect as individuals, in small groups, or in the whole group, the teachers derived scientific meaning and gained understanding from the experience. They shifted their thinking to that of *teachers* of science, considering how to translate their inquiry experiences to their own instructional practices and interactions with students.   ∎

☐ After-School Mathematics Program

At weekly meetings of the After-School Learning Center, researchers, teachers, and teacher educators observed and interacted with students during the first sixty minutes of the session around "thought-revealing activities" in mathematics (Schorr 2004; Schorr & Lesh 2003; Schorr et al. 2007). During the session, students used a sense-making approach to working on complex problems in a collaborative atmosphere. When students left, teachers discussed their own solutions to the problems, along with the students' solutions. They examined mathematical ideas in the problems, related and deeper mathematical ideas, implications for teaching such ideas, and (most important) how they saw the students solve the problems. Through this process, teachers were exposed to a model of mathematics activities that promote understanding and offered opportunities to think about and discuss the instructional implications.   ∎

Focus on Content

Program leaders agree that if teachers are to help students meet challenging mathematics and science standards, the teachers themselves need a strong background in mathematics and science content. Some high school teachers may be sufficiently prepared, but it is likely that elementary, middle, and even some high school teachers will need to strengthen their content knowledge, especially in areas that were not addressed in their preservice preparation.

RESISTANCE TO CONTENT DEVELOPMENT

Unfortunately, some teachers who need content support may not request it. At one end of the spectrum, elementary teachers who have had less than satisfactory experiences in their own mathematics/ science instruction may try to avoid engaging in learning content. At the other end of the spectrum are those high school teachers who consider themselves content experts and may be reluctant to acknowledge gaps in their understanding, even to themselves. For these educators, content-focused professional development remains a "hard sell." In professional development sessions designed to deepen content knowledge, reluctant teachers may divert discussion to logistics, planning, and pedagogy—pursuing any topic except content. The program leader's task is to find ways to provide content-focused professional development in non-threatening situations that enable teachers to see the relevance of the activity.

FOCUS ON BIG IDEAS

Program leaders caution against setting too narrow a content focus. For instance, in grade-level professional development, teachers tend to limit attention to the content they will teach in class. Professional development should challenge teachers to think in terms of what students have learned about the "big ideas" in prior grades, what they are likely to find challenging, and how they will extend the ideas in future years.

☐ Mathematics Assessment

To develop a better understanding of algebraic thinking, conjecture, and proof across the grade levels, a mathematics program focused professional development around publicly released items from the state assessment. After working through the mathematics in assessment items, teachers better understood the goals and expectations of the program. Teachers appreciated the opportunity to encounter mathematical ideas and deepen their own understanding. They also recognized how the mathematics in their program was significant for later experiences their students would have; they could tell what to emphasize and why. This approach provided opportunities to focus on the "big ideas" and mathematical concepts that span grade levels, rather than on day-to-day, incremental bits.   ■

□ "Cognitive Obstacles" in Mathematics Learning

A mathematics program helped teachers understand content better by presenting common obstacles to student understanding. One session for third-grade teachers focused on multiplicative reasoning. The cognitive obstacle that was highlighted was based on a common generalization that teachers might express themselves or that students might develop as they work with basic multiplication facts: "When you multiply two numbers, you get a bigger number." This generalization works for "counting numbers" but not, for example, with zero ($4 \times 0 = 0$), or when negative integers are involved ($4 \times -5 = -20$), or in the case of fractions smaller than one ($4 \times \frac{1}{2} = 2$). This is a case of "overgeneralization." When students carry overgeneralizations with them to new contexts across grades, the new learning cannot be "accommodated" within existing mental constructs (hence a cognitive obstacle exists), and the student experiences disequilibrium. Even though this conundrum is part of the learning process, teachers sometimes hesitate to generate disequilibrium, neglecting to cover the concept in sufficient depth. By focusing on the notion of cognitive obstacles, teachers can recognize and learn more about the dynamics of learning and conceptual understanding.   ■

□ Misconceptions in Science Learning

During professional development in one science program that focused on the content of the student instructional materials, teachers were provided with concrete information about the typical naïve conceptions that students tend to have. Efforts to address teachers' own conceptions, which were often similar to students' misunderstandings, helped teachers learn to avoid promoting student misconceptions in later grades.   ■

Help Teachers Learn to Monitor Student Understanding Through Formative Assessment

Professional development must assist teachers in evaluating whether their mathematics or science instruction is having the desired impact on their students. Sometimes called "formative assessment" (as opposed to summative assessment at the end of a unit), gathering information on student understanding on a continuing basis enables teachers to decide when additional, or different, instruction might be necessary (Black & Wiliam 1998; Stiggins 2005).

Intensive focus on formative assessment typically occurs at the school level, after teachers begin implementing the program. (See Chapter 5.) During more centralized professional development, however, program leaders should introduce formative assessment as an integral part of the improvement initiative and encourage teachers to incorporate this practice in their teaching.

FORMATIVE ASSESSMENT: IDENTIFYING CONCEPTS AND SKILLS

Approaches to professional development that involve formative assessment include:

- Focusing on identifying critical concepts and skills to be assessed and discussing how to collect evidence of student learning (such as through informal questioning or more formal assessment tasks)
- Using formative assessments with pivotal lessons that best reflect the "big ideas" in the unit. Teachers consider posing questions in order to gauge student understanding and inform instructional strategies.
- Verifying that performance assessments in the materials demonstrate "that assessment and instruction go hand-in-hand" and provide evidence to "guide teachers and students toward curricular goals." If the analyses yield deficiencies in the instructional materials' assessments, program leaders should help teachers supplement the assessments.

A WINDOW ON STUDENT THINKING

Teachers using formative assessment were struck by the window it opened into their students' thinking. They appreciated having the opportunity to address identified gaps in student understanding. Teachers also found the process of considering formative assessment helpful in deepening their own content knowledge. Examining items revealed "what we mean by algebraic thinking." Analysis and discussion of student work on the various assessments was particularly helpful, according to program leaders. Scoring performance assessments enabled teachers to "walk in the students' shoes," building a stronger foundation for them to assess students' understanding. In some cases, assessment became "a driving force for teachers to learn more science."

□ Rubrics

Assessment rubrics were developed by a K–8 mathematics program to accompany individual units in student materials. According to the program leader, professional development that was focused on using the rubrics clarified aspects of teaching for understanding:

> This tool helps teachers describe the mathematical understanding that students should develop as a result of engaging in the mathematics unit. The rubrics are also used to set a standard of what students should know and be able to do at each grade level. . . . Through group scoring and discussion of student work, [teachers] are able to move beyond grading only for right and wrong answers to assessing students' mathematical understanding and use of strategies for solving problems.   ■

□ Scoring Institutes

Another K–12 mathematics initiative held "Scoring Institutes" for teachers to examine student work. Each day, the group reflected on evidence of student understanding. After they analyzed the student work, it became clear to teachers and program staff that students were not achieving desired levels of performance. Evidence indicated that students were able to identify a linear pattern but were generally unable to express the mathematics in algebraic terms or to make generalizations when a proof was necessary. What intrigued teachers was the finding that students in grades 8 and 10 demonstrated little growth beyond the understanding demonstrated by the grade 4 students. Teachers began to shift their thinking about what needed to occur in their classrooms to boost mathematical reasoning.   ■

Address Equity Issues and Raise Teacher Expectations of High-Level Mathematics and Science Achievement for All Students

Program leaders advise addressing equity issues as an integral part of professional development. Basically, the challenge is convincing teachers that *all* children can learn powerful, important mathematics and science ideas. The willingness to make changes requires rethinking education at many levels.

A major concern of high school program leaders is raising teacher expectations of students who may not be college-bound. Often teachers indicated that the mathematics and science instructional materials they were being prepared to use were "too advanced" for their "high-risk" students. From these teachers' viewpoint, not all students can or should be enrolled in upper-level mathematics and science courses. As one program leader remarked,

> Because the integrated mathematics curriculum has opened doors for a lot of lower-performing students to take higher levels of mathematics than they ever would have taken before, a number of teachers are not happy when they find some of these students in their higher-level mathematics classes. These teachers don't want the average kid in pre-calculus or calculus class or in some other course from which that kid could have been locked out in the past.

Professional development needs to be designed to enable participating teachers to share and contribute to dialogue and collaboration. Confronting equity concerns in an open atmosphere allows teacher beliefs and assumptions to be brought to light and discussed, with respect and trust.

STRATEGIES TO ADDRESS EQUITY

Strategies to address equity issues include:

- Offering workshops specifically focused on equity issues
- Including students in professional development
- Presenting achievement data from schools that have successfully implemented mathematics and science improvement efforts with at-risk students

☐ Overcoming Low Expectations

A skeptical middle school teacher approached professional development believing that her students were too far behind mathematically to do the activities and that they would become frustrated and quit. She began to change her mind as she observed students participating in the professional development sessions. Students worked on "thought-revealing activities" (see page 32), which were designed as mathematical problems to solve, accompanied by explanations of how they arrived at the solution. Eventually, the teacher challenged one of the professional development providers to visit her classroom and help her implement these kinds of problems. Through an analysis of the videotaped lessons, the teacher learned that her students were, in fact, more capable of higher-level mathematical reasoning than she had originally believed. ∎

☐ Analyzing Lessons

Using a structure called "3 Cs and an E," program leaders worked with teachers to analyze science lessons and ensure rigorous learning opportunities for all students. They analyzed *content* in terms of its appropriateness and connection to standards; *cognitive demand* in terms of the level of thinking required and whether all students were asked to construct deep understanding; *context* in terms of whether the classroom culture was conducive to all students participating at the appropriate level; and *engagement* in terms of how many students were engaged with the lesson at the intended cognitive level. ∎

Designing Site-Based, Job-Embedded Professional Development

5

S ite-based, job-embedded professional development helps participants to implement instructional change in the classroom. School-based professional development lifts teachers out of isolation and promotes dialogue over time among a cross section of teachers—novice and experienced teachers, those who are inclined to change and those who are resistant, etc. Professional development at the school site also helps teachers take ownership of their own professional growth.

Advice shared in previous chapters about designing centralized professional development applies to designing school-based professional development as well. For instance, like centralized professional development, site-based offerings need to strike a balance among content, pedagogy, and instructional materials. A mix of formats helps meet the varied needs of teachers. It is also important to establish and maintain a professional atmosphere of trust and respect, to focus activities around the big ideas embedded in specific instructional materials, and to aid teachers in gauging student understanding as they implement the materials. Additional design specifications for site-based experiences are discussed below.

Create a Culture of Professional Learning at the School

Establishing a culture of professional learning at the school sends teachers the message that the district is serious about implementation. Teachers can expect support as they work to create appropriate learning opportunities for students.

A key component of building a professional learning culture is to provide ample opportunities for teachers to engage in learning activities. Program leaders will probably need to work with both district and school leaders to secure their support and to assist them in finding ways to build in time and opportunities for teacher professional learning. Ideas for ongoing programs include regular grade-level or department meetings focused on teaching and learning, study groups, lesson study, critical friends groups,[4] and coaching and mentoring.

☐ Fall and Spring On-Site Sessions

A K–8 science program held fall and spring afternoon workshops at each school focused on pedagogical issues selected from a menu of options, such as science notebooks. These two-hour events were facilitated by science resource teachers and were designed as follow-up to centralized science kit training. At the end of a long teaching day, having an on-site venue eliminated the usual travel time, and more teachers were willing to participate. They were able to discuss and explore pedagogical issues related to the kits, as well as to learn new strategies to stimulate science learning.   ∎

☐ Study Groups

To support teachers' implementation of instructional materials throughout the school year, several programs set up study groups, which met weekly to monthly at each school. Groups were facilitated by teacher leaders. They provided ongoing opportunities for teachers to discuss their experiences in the classroom in terms of pedagogy, content, and use of instructional materials.   ∎

Empower Teachers Through Networks and Learning Communities

Teacher networks help mold a professional development culture to encourage ongoing learning. In creating "positive subcultures," networks

[4]See the description of the "critical friends" process at the National School Reform Faculty website: www.nsrfharmony.org

can sustain "small pockets of reform" among teachers who are ready to modify their classroom practice.

Cross-Grade and Grade-Level Groups

One strategy to promote school-based learning communities is to structure professional development sessions so that all grade-level teachers in the same school can attend together. Other kinds of teacher networks can be created by structuring time for cross-grade seminars, study groups across schools, and grade-level meetings in school clusters. Cross-grade discussions position content as part of the "big picture"; in contrast, grade-level discussions address more specific content needs in the context of the instructional materials used in the classroom.

☐ Lesson Study

One program leader noted that intensive focus on individual lessons, or "lesson study," fundamentally changed the nature of discussions about mathematics and science content and learning. Groups of three to five teachers worked together in a pre-lesson planning conference, a lesson observation, and a follow-up discussion. Initially, a volunteer teacher described the lesson for that day, its goals, and any issues she or he wanted the group to pay particular attention to during observation of the lesson being taught. The group offered suggestions for refinement and adjustment. By the end of the first year of lesson study, the entire K–8 faculty had participated in three or four sessions. The depth and vibrancy of the sessions varied from group to group, each one reflecting the experience, ideas, and personality of the participants. ∎

☐ Local Learning Communities

A secondary mathematics program facilitated the formation of local learning communities, which were school-based groups of teachers who met and collaborated on issues of mutual interest. A modest amount of funding was provided by the program to plan and implement program-related activities. These learning communities had access to program staff for consultation on an ongoing basis and met several times during the academic year.

In another mathematics program, students were released early once a week so that teachers could plan and participate in school-based staff development. All teachers were required to attend the mathematics network meetings, which were facilitated by teacher leaders or outside consultants. ∎

Provide Coaching and Mentoring Services for Individualized Teacher Support

When sufficient resources are available, strategies such as coaching and mentoring can be extremely effective in improving teacher practice. In the words of a program leader, coaches who provide individualized support can be "at the core of what makes the project successful."

Coaches assist teachers in planning. They observe, provide feedback, and model effective instructional practices. "The coaches have helped me in clarifying where I can improve my teaching methods. They are very positive and non-threatening," said one teacher.

Unintended consequences of using on-site coaches include situations in which coaches get stuck providing logistical support, rather than instruction-focused coaching and mentoring. Administrators or teachers may request that coaches help with materials, ordering, and classroom organization and management. Although these are important tasks, they do not use the valuable knowledge and experience of coaches to the greatest advantage.

Other challenges include identifying highly experienced teachers with the knowledge and skills necessary to serve as coaches. Without this expertise, coaching sessions might result in overly prescriptive or superficial experiences, instead of well-crafted professional development opportunities. Schedule conflicts can also contribute to underutilizing coaches and mentors. Another factor to consider is teachers' apprehension of having their classroom instruction critiqued. These barriers are not insurmountable, but they should be acknowledged and anticipated so that the benefits of coaches can be maximized.

☐ Mathematics Coaches

On-site mathematics coaches worked with K–6 teachers in a program that assigned half of them to support teachers of grades K–2 and the other half to support teachers of grades 3–6. Teachers received monthly visits that consisted of two days of coaching, support, collaborative lesson planning, and/or demonstration lessons. On the first day, each coach brought a substitute teacher to provide a thirty-minute mathematics lesson so that the classroom teacher could work on individual planning. On the second day, coaches assisted teachers, addressing needs identified during the previous coaching session. Typically, support involved modeling of teaching strategies, performing individual student assessment, and side-by-side teaching and assessment.   ∎

☐ Science Coaches

Science resource teachers were assigned sets of elementary schools to work on implementing instructional materials. The resource teachers taught model lessons and provided one-on-one coaching. A program leader noted that this component worked very well:

> One of the major things is having our Science Resource Teachers in the schools with classroom teachers and principals. Our teachers are very comfortable in asking for help and our principals rely upon them greatly to make sure that the kids are getting the science instruction that they need . . . . A large number of our principals are not science-oriented, and having easy access to the Science Resource Teachers is beneficial.   ∎

Ensure the Quality of Site-Based, Job-Embedded Professional Development

Site-based professional development will often be facilitated by school-based personnel. District leaders should take steps to ensure a quality experience for teachers. "It takes artful and experienced facilitation" to push teachers' thinking and to effectively guide the discussion, notes one program leader. With skilled facilitation and well-defined goals, site-based professional development can prove to be very powerful.

Maintaining a high standard of quality can present challenges. If teachers are to learn from study groups or teacher meetings, the sessions must be both structured and facilitated appropriately. The leader of one mathematics professional development program noted that

> It has been challenging to push people's relationships to be more intellectually rigorous. Moving the interactions among teachers and with leaders to the next level is, of course, much more difficult. It requires facilitators and participants to co-create a culture that is not only encouraging and supportive, but also rigorous and reflective. When those facilitators and participants have been long-time colleagues and neighbors, expecting dialogic discourse and the challenging of ideas can be a tall order.

To help ensure the quality of school-based professional development, program leaders recommend using published professional development materials when available. If necessary, program leaders can create their own "tools"; the important point is to provide scaffolds for teacher leaders to use in working with classroom teachers to help ensure quality and consistency.

☐ Focus on Instruction

Program leaders provided a number of tools to help ensure the quality of school-based, job-embedded professional development. These include:

- Videos or cases for teacher discussions
- Guidelines to help teachers frame discussions and share information
- Questions to ask students to elicit their understanding, together with techniques to use student responses as a springboard for professional development related to the teaching and learning process   ■

Part Two: Further Readings

Ball, D. L., & Cohen, D. K. 1999. Developing practice, developing practitioners: Toward a practice-based theory of professional education. In G. Sykes & L. Darling-Hammond (Eds.). *Teaching as the learning profession: Handbook of policy and practice* (pp. 3–32). San Francisco, CA: Jossey-Bass.

Barnett, C., Goldenstein, D., & Jackson, B. 1994. *Fractions, decimals, ratios & percents—Hard to teach and hard to learn?* Portsmouth, NH: Heinemann.

Corcoran, T. B. 1995. *Helping teachers teach well: Transforming professional development* (CPRE Research Briefs Series, RB-16–6/95). New Brunswick, NJ: Consortium for Policy Research in Education.

Elmore, R. F. 1996. Getting to scale with good educational practice. *Harvard Educational Review, 66*(1), 1–26.

Elmore, R. F. 2002. *Bridging the gap between standards and achievement: The imperative for professional development in education.* Washington, DC: Albert Shanker Institute.

Loucks-Horsley, S., Hewson, P. W., Love, N., & Stiles, K. E. 1998. *Designing professional development for teachers of science and mathematics.* Thousand Oaks, CA: Corwin Press.

National Staff Development Council. 2001. *NSDC standards for staff development.* Revised 2001. www.NSDC.org

Smith, M. S. (2001). *Practice-based professional development for teachers of mathematics.* Reston, VA: National Council of Teachers of Mathematics.

Teacher Education Materials Project: A Database for K–12 Mathematics and Science Professional Development Providers. http://www.te-mat.org.

Weiss, I. R. 2006. Professional development and strategic leadership to support effective integration of science and literacy. In R. Douglas, M. P. Klentschy, & K. Worth, with W. Binder (Eds.). *Linking science & literacy in the K–8 classroom* (pp. 359–372). Arlington, VA: National Science Teachers Association Press.

PREPARING PROFESSIONAL DEVELOPMENT PROVIDERS

*T*he previous section distinguished between professional development that is centralized and that which is job-embedded. This section offers advice on preparing professional development providers, both the "provider teams" that will plan and present centralized activities, and the "teacher leaders" who will most likely facilitate school-level activities. In reality, there may well be a great deal of overlap between these two kinds of providers. That is, university and district-level personnel may be involved in planning and presenting school-based professional development, and teacher leaders may facilitate centralized activities. The advice that follows is applicable to professional development providers in either setting.

Part III

6 | Staffing Workshops and Institutes

C areful design of workshops and institutes is necessary, but certainly not sufficient; effective implementation is vital as well. This chapter highlights some key considerations in selecting professional development providers, preparing them for their specific roles, and supporting their efforts over time.

Identify Tasks before Specifying Knowledge and Skills Required of Professional Development Providers

The first step in selecting providers is to identify the tasks expected of them and to differentiate responsibilities and expectations. Making choices is complicated. People implementing professional development as part of an overall mathematics or science education improvement effort may assume myriad responsibilities, including workshop facilitation, one-on-one coaching and mentoring, materials management, parent and community outreach, and advocacy.

Excellent mathematics and science teachers selected to serve as teacher leaders do not necessarily have the requisite skills to take on a full range of responsibilities. In reality, teacher leaders who have proved their effectiveness in the classroom may feel ill at ease taking on new roles as vision-builder, mentor, coach, and advocate. Mathematics and science content experts may experience the reverse situation, lacking the knowledge and skills to help teachers apply what they are learning to their classroom practice. It is important to delineate tasks and responsibilities for each group and to select professional development providers accordingly.

☐ Selection Criteria

One mathematics program identified three categories of professional development providers:

1. Presenters grounded in the instructional materials designated for district use who were well versed in inquiry-based, student-centered pedagogy
2. Experienced teachers to serve as guides or mentors
3. School change consultants to advise and work with school district administrators to plan implementation and address training issues   ■

When Creating Teams, Match Skills and Expertise of Providers

Given the breadth and diversity of roles required of professional development providers, creating provider teams can be highly effective. To meet both content and pedagogical needs of teachers, many programs pair scientists and mathematicians with classroom-savvy teachers. District content specialists or resource teachers contribute knowledge of state and district standards, curricula, and requirements. Pairing "veterans" with less experienced providers can also help build capacity.

☐ Science Teams

Four discipline teams were created to provide professional development in a secondary science program: biology, chemistry, physics, and earth science. For each team, teacher leaders were joined by one or more university faculty members who specialized in the particular discipline. Teams were responsible for developing course outlines for new science units; selecting, developing, or adapting the corresponding instructional materials; developing formative and summative assessments; and preparing science teachers in the district to use the selected materials. Content experts said that teacher leaders helped them gauge the appropriate level at which to instruct teachers in a classroom context, while teacher leaders learned more about content from the scientists.

Other programs grouped providers by making sure each team included at least one highly experienced facilitator. Through this approach, inexperienced professional development providers received on-the-job training.   ∎

Professional Development Providers Need a Shared Vision of High-Quality Mathematics and Science Instruction

The strongest professional development providers have a clear understanding of program vision and goals. Maintaining and fine-tuning a vision of high-quality mathematics and science education that is shared by all is an ongoing leadership task.

Program leaders cannot assume that all teachers with demonstrated expertise in "reform" mathematics and science, or all content experts with experience in K–12 education, have a common vision of high-quality instruction. In retrospect, mathematics and science program leaders realized they should have "assumed nothing." In other cases, program leaders found that providers shared a vision of high-quality classroom instruction, but not the professional development needed to create this kind of instruction.

RECONCILING DIFFERENCES

Especially when professional development teams include both content experts and teacher leaders, it is important to reconcile conflicting visions of quality education. People with different prior experiences may hold different views about classroom instruction. Even district programs with a long history of working with university faculty on teacher enhancement programs are not immune to such tensions. One K–8 science program leader reported that serious conflict arose between teacher leaders and science partners during the first summer institute, resulting in feelings of resentment among teacher leaders that "took years to overcome." Clearly, some "up front" work on a shared vision is worthwhile.

SUSTAINING THE VISION

Sustaining the program vision over time can be difficult, especially as new providers are brought in to assist. "The more we try to scale up and bring teacher leaders to do the professional development, the harder it is to maintain a shared vision," one program leader remarked. In another case, core program staff achieved a shared vision of high-quality science education; however, the vision did not transfer to school-based leaders, who had been less involved in the initial planning and program discussions.

Similarly, maintaining a common vision became more difficult when consultants were brought in by a program to provide mathematics expertise. Differences in philosophy and approach to professional development were evident. Program leaders had to stop midway and spend time negotiating between teacher leaders and content specialists to create common ground and expectations.

☐ Shared Vision Strategies

Program samplers for maintaining project vision and goals include:

- Involving all providers in designing professional development. One science program teamed each content expert with a teacher leader and another classroom teacher to co-plan the content courses, focusing on important science concepts from the student instructional materials.

- A K–8 science program prepared teacher leaders through an initial three-day workshop to fashion a shared vision of effective science teaching and learning, followed by a three-week leadership academy.

Other strategies included planning annual retreats for providers, regular meetings among program partners, and monthly school site meetings. ∎

☐ Model the Model

In one project, college faculty members were recruited to scale up a professional development effort to teach science via a "model the model" approach. Co-planning, followed by co-teaching and collegial mentoring, helped build a common vision of inquiry-based science instruction. A human biology course for K–5 teachers was led by a science education faculty member whose course design infused the content with inquiry pedagogy. In addition, the program leader involved a member of the Biology Department in planning and teaching a course that would model inquiry in the sciences. The two academics spent many hours together outlining the course and examining the guides that local teachers were using in human biology. They taught the course to rave reviews. The following year, they recruited the Biology Department chair at the local community college, who was well versed in content but accustomed to lecturing in fifty-minute chunks rather than using a more diverse set of instructional strategies. The three-member team revised the original course and co-taught it. The science educator served as a mentor to his fellow team members, and the more experienced pair took turns co-teaching and bringing the "new kid" aboard with structured inquiry.   ■

Ensure That the Professional Development Team Has Adequate Mathematics and Science Content Knowledge

Effective teachers need both subject matter knowledge and pedagogical content knowledge. Subject matter knowledge consists of understanding the mathematics and science concepts, as well as the methods and principles that guide study in these disciplines. Pedagogical content knowledge includes an understanding of student thinking and the ability to draw on a repertoire of ways to represent specific mathematics and science concepts so that they are comprehensible to others (Shulman 1986).

Providers of institute- or workshop-type professional development must not only understand subject matter covered in student instructional materials; they also must have an understanding of, and be able to articulate, the "big content picture"—that is, how the content in the instructional materials fits into the curriculum as a whole. As noted above, many mathematics and science programs have addressed this issue by creating provider teams that include "content experts," in many cases mathematics and science faculty from local colleges and universities. Often, however, districts must rely on teacher leaders to provide much of the professional development. This is the "really challenging piece" for many programs: working with teacher leaders on developing awareness of content strands over the course of grades K–12.

Leaders of mathematics and science education programs report that the "content knowledge problem" often surfaces during professional development sessions as teacher leaders try to help teachers make sense of the content of student instructional materials. One program leader observed that even though each professional development session focused on a single mathematical strand, the activities often lacked the "connective tissue needed to help participants see the 'big ideas' of the strand." Program leaders concluded that teacher leaders are likely to need substantial opportunities to deepen their own conceptual understanding of mathematics or science, which may include content institutes, graduate coursework, online courses, and a support network for reflection and debriefing on the content.

☐ Developing Conceptual Storylines

A two-day meeting was held for providers in an elementary science program to articulate the science content goals and "conceptual storylines" for each institute. The program provided teacher leaders with outside content experts as coaches, and the teacher leaders met monthly to prepare for and debrief workshops. During the meeting, they worked to develop "increasingly stronger and more content-focused conceptual storylines, as well as training scripts that included reference to the storylines." ■

☐ Professional Development Materials

Commercially available professional development materials can also help providers acquire content knowledge. In one program, teachers on special assignment used *Physics by Inquiry* materials, which provided content as well as pedagogical strategies designed to help participants "learn and practice how to guide teachers in developing their own operational definitions of the essential science concepts" (McDermott 1996). Other programs used *Developing Mathematical Ideas*, a professional development curriculum designed for teacher leaders to examine the major ideas of K–6 mathematics and how children develop those ideas (Schifter et al. 2000). At the secondary level, program leaders used *The Fostering Algebraic Thinking Toolkit* (Driscoll et al. 2001). These programs were effective tools for professional development, and they spared program leaders the task of creating their own professional development materials. ■

☐ Coursework

A secondary mathematics program initially provided teacher leaders with training in content at a two-day session in the spring, a three-day summer institute, and teacher leadership seminars during the school year. When observations revealed a continuing need to strengthen teacher leaders' content knowledge, program staff designed a number of online courses to supplement their face-to-face efforts.

Some program leaders advocate formal coursework for teacher leaders, conducted by university professors who not only understand content, but also share the program's view of quality instruction. In a K–12 mathematics program, a district mathematics coordinator recruited teachers who were already emerging as leaders to enroll in a master's of education program that became "an unintended training ground for many of the district's teacher leaders." ∎

Build in Opportunities for Providers to Gain Expertise in Pedagogy

Before they can effectively help others, professional development providers need to learn and practice instructional strategies that facilitate learning. In particular, scientists and mathematicians who serve as content experts may have limited experience in using pedagogies other than a lecture-demonstration method of teaching. Insufficient preparation to model effective pedagogy can result in providers who "talk the talk," but do not "walk the walk." Leaders of mathematics and science education programs report that mathematicians and scientists, as well as teacher leaders, often encounter difficulty with important pedagogical practices, including "subtly and skillfully questioning to further understanding, effectively drawing out and challenging misconceptions, and fostering expansive dialogue."

Experiencing the professional development first as learners helps prepare providers to work with teachers. Program leaders recommend this approach, as scaffolding the work of professional development providers can develop the knowledge and skills necessary for facilitating high-quality professional development and can help them anticipate how others might engage with the materials.[5]

☐ Understanding "Best Practices"

One mathematics improvement program involved a partnership among several institutions of higher education and ten school districts focused on the development of teachers' mathematical content knowledge. University partners planned to develop a series of six

---

[5]For a collection of reviews of published professional development materials, see www.te-mat.org

mathematics content courses for teachers to take over three sum-mers. At the first planning meeting, the K–12 partners made it clear that the summer institute content courses should not be "more of the same" courses that teachers experienced in teacher preparation pro-grams. Instead, these new courses should model "best practices" for K–12 mathematics instruction. When confronted with this demand, university partners were confused: What is the meaning of "best prac-tices"? Program leaders responded with a workshop for university staff on best practices in K–12 mathematics education, which turned out to be a great success. ■

☐ Observation Lessons

Leaders of a science education program perceived a need to improve pedagogical practices of professional development providers. They used observation lessons, in which prospective providers observed teaching practice; then they discussed and reflected on the experi-ence. Other improvement measures included meetings organized around the pedagogy of inquiry-based science, which incorporated modeling of lessons followed by debriefing. National workshops, such as The Institute for Inquiry offered by the Exploratorium, were highly recommended for providing in-depth experiences in pedagogy for professional development providers.[6] ■

Provide Ongoing Support for Professional Development Providers

Like teachers, professional development providers need ongoing sup-port. The need for continuing support is especially important when providers take on unfamiliar professional development roles. If they are to maintain their motivation and continue to improve and learn from one another, providers need time to meet and to reflect on their work. An integrated system for both preparing and supporting pro-fessional development providers is helpful, including formal and in-formal meetings, institutes and conferences, co-teaching with peers, mentoring by core staff and master teachers, study group research, and development of teaching "scripts" for workshops.

Program leaders caution that it is particularly difficult to find time to provide the necessary support for teacher leaders who continue to

[6]For more information on The Exploratorium programs, see www.exploratorium.edu/ifi/workshops/index.html

work as classroom teachers. As new providers join the team, planning activities that meet everyone's needs is yet another challenge. The leader of a K–8 science program commented,

> A major challenge of the project was to find significant professional growth provider time for both planning and reflection . . . Another challenge was that after 10 years of monthly leadership meetings, it became more and more difficult to meet the highly diverse needs in new and interesting ways. Sessions could become repetitive, and diversity of the group became more extreme as time passed. Many of the elementary science lead teachers, for instance, had more than 70 monthly meetings and five summer institutes, while others had just joined the group.

☐ Staff Support Strategies

Program leaders have devised a variety of mechanisms for providing ongoing support to professional development providers:

- Regular staff meetings improve communication, providing opportunities to discuss problems and devise solutions to implementation barriers. One program had weekly meetings with staff developers and bi-weekly meetings with site-based teacher leaders, staff developers, and the program leader.

- "Communities of learners" provide mutual support and enhance teacher leaders' appreciation and capacity for life-long learning. Providers participate in multi-day training sessions and planning meetings, as well as debriefing activities after professional development sessions. As the cadre of teacher leaders develops, they function as a support group and learning community. ∎

Staffing On-Site Professional Development | 7

*T*his chapter serves as a guide to planning job-embedded professional development at the school site level. Teacher leaders are likely to facilitate this work, and district administrators need to pay attention to identifying, preparing, and supporting candidates for these critical positions. Teacher leaders not only increase the pool of available providers but also help build district capacity to scale up and maintain the mathematics/science improvements efforts.

Establish Multiple Levels of Teacher Leadership

Many mathematics and science education initiatives support cadres of teachers to assist in providing professional development. "Teachers on special assignment" may be released from their classroom responsibilities to serve as facilitators, mentors, and coaches; in other cases, programs hire retired teachers to serve in these roles. Programs often involve school-based teacher leaders who continue fulfilling their classroom teaching responsibilities while serving as liaisons between central program staff and teachers in their building. Teacher leaders are also involved in developing and piloting materials and assessments and in providing support through in-school networks.

PRACTICAL LEADERSHIP

Teacher leaders provide "practical leadership" for professional development initiatives. Said one,

> What I do on a daily basis can help people move toward the purpose I am working toward. I am activating different parts of the network in which I move. I can have a conversation in the hallway and activate that part of the network. I can talk to the principal or go to a district meeting. [Leadership happens] in the ways I act every day, but keeping the larger purpose in mind in the things I choose to do. [Practical leadership] is teachers using their influence on an everyday basis.

☐ Organizational Models of Teacher Leadership

One K–8 science program used two kinds of teacher leaders:

Science Resource Teachers
- designed and implemented professional development
- provided classroom coaching and mentoring
- provided resources for classroom teachers
- worked with principals

Lead Science Writing Teachers
- worked with Science Resource Teachers to develop new strategies for teaching expository writing in science to strengthen students' conceptual understanding and science process skills, while also improving writing skills

Another program developed a multi-level teacher leadership structure. Some teachers provided professional development, another group pilot-tested materials, and a third group focused on developing professional learning communities within the schools.

Still another example of a multi-level teacher leadership model involved three groups.

- Group 1: District resource teachers presented professional development and served as liaisons between the central office and individual schools.
- Group 2: Teacher leaders led teacher meetings and served as informal resources for other teachers in their schools.
- Group 3: School-based coaches modeled lessons, facilitated grade-level meetings, and encouraged teachers to participate in professional development. ∎

Be Strategic in Recruiting Teacher Leaders from Existing Networks

Recruiting teacher leaders from existing networks may seem logical, but this approach may also have disadvantages. Those teacher leaders selected from the ranks of district mathematics or science committees or on the basis of a principal's recommendation may well have other responsibilities that compete for their attention. It's also wise to take into consideration that criteria used by school or district administrators to appoint teacher leaders may differ from those used by mathematics and science education leaders.

CRITERIA FOR SELECTING TEACHER LEADERS

If they are to recommend candidates, administrators need to be apprised of what programs are looking for in a teacher leader; everyone should be on the same page. An object lesson from a K–8 science program underscores the significance of briefing administrators. In this case, principals recommended candidates on the grounds that the program would be good for the teachers' own professional growth. The program leader remarked, "There was no consistency of what the expectations were for those teachers." In another program in which principals selected teacher liaisons, a program leader reflected, "We should have been much more proactive in the selection of the leaders" and "spent more time with principals in the beginning and explained to them what we wanted."

Here are criteria that one program used to identify teacher leaders to serve as middle school mathematics mentor teachers:

- Exemplary mathematics teaching practices
- Experience in professional development delivery
- Experience with peer coaching techniques
- Knowledge of standards-based instructional programs

SCREENING FOR LEADERSHIP EXPERIENCE

Candidates for teacher leadership positions in a middle school mathematics program were selected by school administrators and the district mathematics coordinator on the basis of

- Leadership potential
- Interest and commitment to the improvement of mathematics education
- Availability and willingness to serve as teacher leaders

However teacher leaders are recruited, program leaders should participate in the final selection. In one program that suggested selection criteria for teacher leaders, yet relied on schools to make the final choices, few of the teacher leaders had the requisite experience in leadership roles. Those who had leadership experience "often came with make-and-take images of professional development," rather than the program vision of in-depth, content-rich professional development.

☐ Application and Selection Process

In the search for K–8 science teacher leaders who were "in synch" with program goals and vision, one program incorporated the principals' recommendations but did not rely on them exclusively. An application process asked teachers to do three things:

- Write an essay with specific components
- Submit two letters of recommendation (one of which had to be from the principal)
- Participate in an interview by program staff ∎

Provide Initial Guidelines for Teacher Leaders, but Be Prepared for the Work to Evolve over Time

Providing initial guidelines helps teacher leaders to focus their work and gauge their progress. Without direction, teacher leaders may feel overwhelmed, frustrated, and inefficient. Instead of being "thrown into the lion's den," teacher leaders need direction up front. However, defining the work too rigidly should also be avoided. One program leader suggests setting up a "common vision" for teacher leaders, rather than a "common program."

Over time, teacher leaders become more comfortable with their work and begin to identify what is needed to help the improvement effort. One program leader describes this process:

> At first, [teacher leaders] worked with teacher trainers. They came out of the classroom for a day to lead a professional development. . . . Now, they do lots of school committee presentations, [they] meet with curriculum administrators in schools to work out the workshops they need at the school-level, and they spend more time in classrooms. Their role has changed; it is a difference in their comfort level being in classrooms and exerting that role.

Table 1 Program Roles and Responsibilities

Teacher Leaders	Classroom Teachers
Discuss needs-based issues with classroom teachers	Meet with teacher leaders to share needs
Help teachers implement adopted science curricula	Attend school-based meetings; participate in peer coaching
Model strategies for teaching hands-on science	Request teacher leaders to model instruction
Provide science content background information	Communicate about unfamiliar content
Assist with classroom and district science performance-based assessment	Work with teacher leaders on classroom assessment

☐ Defining Teacher Leader Roles

In one program, teacher leaders developed their own job descriptions after feeling frustrated in trying to figure out their roles. Because everyone in the group was enrolled in a specially designed graduate class, a university faculty member helped them define their leadership roles.

Another program shaped the work of teacher leaders around a framework that clarified the roles and responsibilities of teacher leaders and of the classroom teachers with whom they worked. (See Table 1.)   ■

Prepare Teacher Leaders to Work with Adult Learners

Leaders of past improvement efforts report that in the effort to prepare teacher leaders in content and pedagogy, they neglected essential skills needed for facilitation, coaching, and mentoring roles. It should not be assumed that teacher leaders already know how to communicate with their peers as adult learners. One program director observed that many teacher leaders didn't think of themselves as "teachers of teachers" and were uncomfortable presuming to know more than their colleagues. A program evaluator noted that teacher leaders "find it difficult to switch gears and think like adult educators." The result was that teacher leaders sometimes "talked down" to their colleagues in training sessions or treated them "just like the kids." Some may also find it difficult to address the different learning styles and needs of individual teachers.

Teachers who are providing ongoing leadership within their schools in turn need ongoing support to help them clarify their roles and obtain feedback to strengthen their efforts. Said one program leader, "[Teacher leaders] need some kind of support and understanding to facilitate their experience. They don't automatically know what they need." Another program leader echoed this theme: "A professional group for the lead teachers is critical; they need a regular place and a point person to always meet with to share successes and challenges."

☐ Training for Teacher Leaders

A middle school mathematics improvement program provided teacher leaders with training in cognitive coaching (Costa & Garmston 2002) as well as workshop presentation strategies. Teacher leaders presented a workshop and used the cognitive coaching model of holding a pre-conference with their partner (for this purpose, the partner was actually the coach). After observing the workshop, the partner held a post-conference with the teacher leader to share feedback.

Another program offered training in the form of a three-credit graduate course on teacher leadership. Participants also met every Friday for five years to plan their work, discuss concerns, and solve problems.

In a similar example, a graduate class of teacher leaders met once a week to examine national education reform, the nature of adult learners, and stages of change, as well as to discuss issues related to their immediate needs.

Other professional development programs included a component for teacher leaders that helped them "organize their practical knowledge." In one case, teacher leaders co-taught a science methods course with a university faculty member. In another, teacher leaders met regularly for training on such topics as cognitive coaching, facilitating collaborative groups, improving presentations, and working with resistors. ■

Expect to Take Years, Rather Than Months, to Fully Prepare Teacher Leaders

For teachers to become fully competent teacher leaders, they will need to participate in a variety of high-quality learning opportunities over a period of years. In retrospect, program directors who relied on teacher leaders acknowledged they did not pay enough attention to preparing and supporting them. The issue is a thorny one, as pressures to scale up may force teacher leaders to begin their work before they are fully prepared and to learn on the job. Those who have led improvement efforts, however, advise district supervisors to work with teacher leaders as long as possible before having the teacher leaders serve as providers. It is especially important to involve them in reviewing instructional materials and planning professional development.

Offer Incentives and Support to Encourage Potential Teacher Leaders

Even though teacher leadership is critical, it can be burdensome for teachers who continue to teach full-time or who find the pressures of leadership daunting. If too much is expected of them, teacher leaders may quickly burn out. Programs that did not offer sufficient incentives and support to teacher leaders found that leadership was difficult to sustain. One K–8 science program investigated the causes of the high turnover they were experiencing in their school-based leadership cadre. They found that teachers did not want to take time away from their classrooms and that they tried to fulfill their obligations at the end of the school day, quickly leading to burnout. Most of them were unwilling to commit to more than one year of service. As the program leader remarked,

> We have to develop strategies to support, entice, motivate, and reward people who step up to be leaders or advocates or whatever we want to call them. . . . Rewards can be release time, status, money.

Implement an Ongoing Recruitment Process to Respond to Both Staff Turnover and Scale-Up Demands

Recruiting teacher leaders should begin in advance of the program's debut and continue as the program expands. In addition, program leaders should anticipate that training teachers as leaders will create new opportunities for these individuals, both within and outside the district.

Program leaders were often surprised at the high turnover rate of teacher leaders. Once teachers were trained as leaders to deliver professional development, district administrators recognized their talents and often promoted them to leadership roles outside of mathematics and science. All of a sudden, programs found they were short on teacher leaders. Over the life span of one mathematics program, three of four middle school teacher leaders became administrators or professional development providers in neighboring school districts; the fourth retired and continued to work with other school districts as a part-time mathematics consultant.

When asked what to expect in terms of long-term staffing, program leaders were frank: anticipate and plan for a shortage of teacher leaders—expect high levels of attrition due to job fatigue and teacher leader mobility.

☐ Recruitment Strategies

Approaches to recruitment include leadership seminars and other formal professional development opportunities, such as teacher leadership discussion groups, to recruit teachers interested in co-leading workshops.

In the early stages of one initiative, program leaders identified potential teacher leaders during introductory workshops and classroom visits. Their selection criteria included teacher interest, knowledge, and readiness to engage in teacher leadership. Other professional development programs found that "regular" teachers emerged as leaders out of school-based learning communities that were part of those programs.

A K–8 science program had success asking Teachers on Special Assignment to recruit school-based leaders informally. Teachers who demonstrated interest and skill were encouraged to apply. They also asked principals to identify prospective teacher leaders. "We find the one-to-one recruitment with candidates who have promising qualities is the best method," reflects one program leader.　　　■

In Choosing Teacher Leaders, Consider a Range of Skills, Expertise, and Viewpoints

Teacher leaders can play an influential role in improving classroom practice. Their credibility with other teachers hinges on successful prior teaching experience, including experience with the instructional materials to be used in the classroom. These teacher leaders can reassure teachers who think the instructional materials will be too difficult for students, because their expertise enables them to "provide concrete assistance to teachers, and speak knowledgeably about what students were able to do with the material."

On the other hand, program leaders suggest that districts also include as teacher leaders people who are not necessarily the most knowledgeable in content or the best at teaching mathematics or science, but who are considered leaders by their peers. "If you don't win those people over," one program leader says, "you're dead in the water."

In addition, there are times when less experienced teachers turn out to be strong teacher leaders. When a secondary mathematics program was short on applicants, all teachers who applied were accepted as teacher leaders. To their surprise, program leaders found that "the leadership team members whose involvement we questioned at the beginning . . . became the most effective leaders in the program. This speaks to the untapped potential that rests below the surface and is identifiable only by providing opportunities for such people to step forward."

Part Three: Further Readings

Carroll, C., & Mumme, J. 2007. *Learning to lead mathematics professional development.* Thousand Oaks, CA: Corwin Press and WestEd.

Lord, B., Cress, K., & Miller, B. 2003. Teacher leadership as classroom support: The challenge of scale and feedback in mathematics and science education reform. Newton, MA: Education Development Center.

Stein, M. K., Smith, M. S., & Silver, E. A. 1999. The development of professional developers: Learning to assist teachers in new settings in new ways. *Harvard Education Review, 69,* 237–269.

West, L., & Staub, F. C. 2003. *Content-focused coaching: Transforming mathematics lessons.* Portsmouth, NH: Heinemann.

BUILDING A SUPPORTIVE SYSTEM

*P*rior sections of this book have emphasized the importance of setting a vision and goals, adopting a professional stance toward teachers as change agents, designing appropriate professional development, and preparing teacher leaders and other providers to facilitate professional learning activities. This section offers advice on making the improvement effort an ongoing part of the system. Changing the system will involve developing a culture of shared responsibility for student learning that takes into account—but goes beyond—existing accountability pressures on schools. Also included is advice on systematically building support among administrators and the broader community, and other ways to plan for sustainability.

8 | *Measuring and Reporting Progress*

"If teachers implement this program, will test scores improve?" When asked about impact on student test scores, program leaders need to communicate the value of moving beyond test-based accountability to taking responsibility for student learning so that the question becomes *"What must I do to help students achieve the mathematics and science learning goals?"*

In the current "high-stakes" climate, pressure for high test scores is a reality. Part of the challenge for leaders of mathematics and science education initiatives is to demonstrate that student learning is improving, both on state assessments and on other measures that may reflect more dimensions of achievement.

Share Responsibility for Student Learning System-Wide

Educators at all levels of the system must take responsibility for helping students meet learning goals. District leaders must provide the necessary resources for mathematics and science instruction. They must also make certain that principals (1) understand and support teachers' efforts to improve instruction, and (2) follow through to confirm that teachers are applying what they are learning in the professional development to their classrooms. Program leaders can work with school boards to ensure that they are familiar with the improvement effort and its learning goals and to encourage board members to visit schools and request regular progress reports.

Likewise, principals must be responsible for what happens at the school level. They need to ensure that the instructional materials designated for classroom use are implemented as intended. Program leaders can assist principals by providing tools to strengthen implementation. As noted in Chapter 4, teachers can assume more responsibility for student learning by regularly assessing student progress toward learning goals and adjusting instruction accordingly.

☐ Learning Walks

Some mathematics and science education leaders have found ways to support district and school personnel in these responsibilities by providing tools for gathering data. For example, in one district that used "Learning Walks" (Bloom 2007) to check on the quality of instruction in all subjects, program leaders helped principals and central office staff consider in advance what high-quality mathematics instruction would look like, using observation forms to help guide them. According to the program leader, the fact that these forms were widely used by the principals in their classroom observations "clearly communicated to teachers and students that standards-based instruction was valued."   ∎

☐ School Report Card

Another common strategy for accountability at the school level is the use of a "school report card." A leader of an elementary mathematics program, for example, described how the report cards in some participating schools had changed to better reflect the kinds of learning taking place, focusing on multiple criteria, not just on a single grade. Another program leader reported that a generalized report card for grades K–5 was revised to consist of a series of report cards specific to each grade. Details of student achievement were reported, including each student's mastery of specific content ideas and process skills. Program leaders noted that their report cards not only were an accountability device for the students but also increased the likelihood that the teacher would feel obligated to teach the indicated science kits. If information was missing, parents usually wanted to know why.

Another program held teachers accountable for a high standard of instruction by having them share their students' mathematics work and discuss student progress in regularly scheduled meetings. This strategy highlighted the expectation that all teachers would follow the recommended curriculum sequence with all of their students. Others talked about the need for an organized structure for tracking, documenting, and reporting levels of classroom implementation linked to state standards. These approaches, and others like them, send clear messages to teachers and principals that the district is serious about improving mathematics and science education and that everyone is expected to support that effort.   ■

Address Teachers' Accountability Concerns

Teachers may be in agreement with the vision of teaching and learning inherent in a mathematics or science program; however, they need to reconcile their practice with the pressure to prepare their students for high-stakes assessments. Program leaders must acknowledge the "realities of accountability." Helping teachers to discern the alignment between student learning goals and state assessments is one approach, along with embedding appropriate test-taking strategies into the instructional materials. As one leader explained, "effective instruction includes sound test-taking strategies, not 'test prep,' and prepares students for testing but does not dominate teaching time."

Some program leaders advise addressing teacher concerns by modeling and discussing ways to balance teaching facts with teaching for understanding. Others assist teachers in interpreting test results, using the analysis to improve teaching and learning. Explaining the links between the instructional strategies that teachers are being asked to use and state/local performance standards is another important strategy. As one leader noted,

> You can't ignore [high-stakes testing]. Teachers are concerned. . . . [You need to] give them strategies to work with, and encourage them to trust that the content and pedagogy will prevail in the test scores.

☐ Alignment with Science Assessments

Program leaders in an elementary science initiative worked with teachers to address misconceptions regarding the degree to which instructional materials were aligned with the state assessments.

Rumors that the materials did a poor job of preparing students for the state assessments did not mesh with the experiences of program personnel. To address this issue, program leaders designed professional development to show teachers how to use the instructional materials to prepare students for the state assessments. They also developed additional science support materials that clearly demonstrated this overall alignment, suggested supplementary activities to address any gaps, identified important vocabulary, and showed teachers how to promote language development through science instruction. ∎

☐ Alignment with State Learning Goals

In one school district, educators were required to justify their choice of classroom activities by demonstrating correlation with state standards and making the case that students' performance on the state assessment would improve. The science initiative in this district related the science kit materials to state standards during professional development sessions. Program leaders went to great lengths to supplement each kit with support materials that showed how kit activities addressed the state standards for science, as well as those for language arts and mathematics. ∎

☐ Exam Questions

Leaders of another professional development effort developed a "Standardized Exam Preparation Resource," a database that correlated exam preparation questions with specific mathematical curriculum units. The goal was to help teachers recognize that the instructional materials would prepare their students for the high-stakes tests without their having to resort to "test prep." ∎

☐ Rethinking "Test Preparation"

Still another program developed a resource to help teachers rethink the way they prepared their students to take standardized examinations. In the past, many teachers had spent weeks, if not months, preparing students for exams. Staff developers helped teachers connect units of study to standardized test content. By embedding test preparation into units of study, they found that students and teachers were making more direct connections between content in the curriculum and its presentation on standardized tests. ∎

Examine State and District Assessments and Address Any Mismatches with the Program Vision of High-Quality Mathematics and Science Education

In the long run, many stakeholders will judge the program by student performance results. So it is important for program leaders to be proactive in addressing any misalignment between the program vision and state/district assessments. Some programs have the good fortune of working with high-stakes assessments that reflect the direction in mathematics and science instruction they support. More often, however, program leaders are confronted with state and district assessments that measure learning of mathematics and science knowledge and skills different from those they would like to emphasize.

Program leaders must understand and communicate what standardized assessments can and cannot measure with regard to program effects, and they must educate stakeholders about other measures of student learning that may be more closely aligned with the student learning goals established by the program.

Some program leaders address the alignment issue by administering additional tests that are nationally known and reasonably in line with the program goals. However, in some cases, resistance to administering additional tests because of the time and expense involved can be an obstacle. In such situations, program leaders in mathematics and science education have few choices but to use the tests already in place and make their best effort to communicate about both the merits and the shortcomings of the resulting evidence.

☐ Using Existing Assessments

Students enrolled in high school integrated mathematics courses were required to take state exit exams for Algebra I and Algebra II. Although these tests were not aligned with the content of the integrated mathematics courses, these students performed at least as well as students who had taken traditional algebra courses. These results were more convincing to stakeholders than if program leaders had designed their own test to demonstrate the value of the integrated mathematics sequence.   ■

☐ Classroom-Based Assessment

Some district leaders used measures they developed themselves, under the title "classroom-based assessment systems." With these measures in place, results could be communicated to a variety of stakeholders, including teachers, students and their parents/guardians. Classroom assessment data enabled program leaders to better assess program impact and to ensure that the program maintained an ongoing focus on student achievement. One program leader explained that "the district now has a quarterly assessment system in place utilizing assessments from the curriculum," noting that this alignment of assessment and curriculum is critical for long-term support of the program.   ∎

Gather Data and Communicate Results for a Broad Range of Outcomes

It is important to monitor and communicate student learning results throughout the effort, but using such results too early to judge the effectiveness of the improvement effort can lead to erroneous conclusions. It takes time to improve teaching and learning. Teachers need to gain new knowledge and skills first, next apply what they have learned to their classrooms, and then refine their practice.

Program leaders should gather data on a range of outcomes, including some that should show evidence in a short time frame and others (such as improved student achievement) that will take longer. Studies might examine:

- The impact of professional development on the establishment of learning communities within and across schools
- The impact on teachers' professional learning and growth (for instance, the number of teachers seeking National Board certification or assuming leadership positions)
- The impact on classroom practice
- Student and parent response to changes
- The impact on student interest in mathematics and science
- The impact on student knowledge and skills

ATTRIBUTING GAINS TO PROGRAM ACTIVITIES

Ascribing gains to program activities can be challenging. For instance, a district cannot declare professional development a success just because students scored higher on a test at the end of the year than they did at the start. Students are expected to learn over the course of a school year, whether or not their teachers participated in professional development. Similarly, data indicating that a district scored higher than the state average on a mathematics or science assessment may not serve as valid evidence of impact. Program leaders need to be able to make the case that a positive result can be attributed to the professional development program and is not merely an artifact of demographic differences. Program leaders, therefore, need to think through strategies for gathering data that will relate program activities—such as teacher professional development—to improved student achievement.

BE PREPARED WITH DATA

"Be prepared with data" is the message, especially for those who make the decisions about how much and what kinds of professional development will be offered. As one program leader explained, "Administrators appear supportive, but with the high stakes involved in state-level standardized testing, they will expect to see improved test scores within a reasonable time frame." It is evidence of impacts on student test scores that will move district decision makers toward sustained support for the mathematics or science program.

☐ Student Achievement Data

One program gained support when leaders were able to show that "the improvements in student achievement and the reductions in the gap are clearly related to the intensity of the professional development program. The schools in which teachers took fewer hours of professional development and/or made teacher participation voluntary showed lower gains."

Another program leader reported an initial reluctance among many teachers and administrators to implement the mathematics instructional materials "because of the fear that student performance would decline." When the program evaluation found that students in "strong implementation classrooms" were performing at much higher levels on the state test, particularly in the problem-solving domain, the result was "paradigm shifts among upper-level administrative staff, principals, and teachers." The fact that the greatest gains were made by Hispanic, African American, and economically disadvantaged students was particularly important in generating support for the program.   ■

☐ Literacy Gains

Because of a strong focus on language arts in state assessment programs, a number of initiatives have found it helpful to show that their efforts in mathematics and science resulted in improved student achievement in reading and writing. For example, one program "provided evidence to substantiate the hypothesis that inquiry science is an excellent context for language development in students who are not native speakers of English. Students participating in three consecutive [program] summer schools showed significant increases in both science understanding and language development." ■

☐ Student Enrollment in Higher-Level Courses

One high school mathematics program gathered data on the percentage of students enrolling in higher-level mathematics courses. African American and Hispanic students, in particular, were taking advanced courses in greater numbers. Program leaders also made plans to follow students into college, monitoring their SAT performance and their success in mathematics courses. ■

☐ Elementary Science Achievement

In order to demonstrate that the district's significant investment in teacher enhancement was worthwhile, some programs linked student test data directly to professional development. One K–8 science program demonstrated a significant positive relationship between the amount of time teachers at a school spent on professional development and the percentage of grade 5 students who met the science standard on the state test. In addition, data from a national science assessment showed that schools implementing the practices promoted by the program were more successful than non-implementing schools at meeting the needs of students classified as eligible for free or reduced-price lunch.

Another K–8 science initiative used Partnership for the Assessment of Standards-Based Science (PASS) assessments to demonstrate longitudinal, positive change in fifth-grade student scores and understanding.[7] Among the key findings:

1. Program students outperformed students from similar socioeconomic backgrounds in all categories.
2. The students who gained the most were students of color, suggesting that hands-on science is an effective way to reach all students.

[7]For more information on PASS, see www.wested.org/cs/we/ view/pj/278

3. Those students whose teachers participated in one hundred or more hours of professional development in the first three years scored higher in the open-ended response section, which may be attributable to the use of science notebooks. ■

CONNECTIONS BETWEEN PROGRAM COMPONENTS AND IMPROVED STUDENT LEARNING

In addition to sharing outcomes of the overall improvement effort, it is critical for program leaders to design measures that will make the connection between *specific* program activities and improved student learning. Emphasizing the benefits of program activities can be a proactive way of justifying aspects of the initiative that are particularly expensive and time-consuming. When resources are tight—as they usually are in school districts—decision makers will be tempted to cut back on key program activities unless there is sufficient evidence that the activities are contributing to improvements.

Building and Sustaining Support for Mathematics and Science Education Improvement

S uggestions outlined in earlier sections of this book lay the foundation for creating and sustaining support for improvement in mathematics and science education. Establishing a vision at the highest level of administration and setting professional development goals are key. Devoting time and energy to working collaboratively with teachers and developing teacher leadership are essential steps to move the program forward and improve teaching and learning.

There's still more to be done in service of system-wide support for mathematics and science improvement. The list includes building support among administrators and parents, tapping into the mathematics and science community, and initiating a sustainability plan.

Define Roles and Expectations of District and School Administrators

To survive within the chaotic world of districts and schools, program leaders need to spell out what they want administrators to do, particularly with regard to providing resources and assigning teachers to participate in improvement efforts. In light of competing and sometimes conflicting initiatives that may capture administrators' attention, a shared understanding is essential. Program leaders advised being explicit from the very start. Agreements detailing roles and responsibilities should be in writing.

Just as district administrators need a solid understanding of what commitment to the program entails, principals need to understand the nature of their involvement. It is important to clarify that principals must do more than "give teachers permission to participate." Principals should invest their own professional development time in becoming familiar with the initiative. They need to provide resources and support structures for their teachers, and to engage them through classroom observation and dialogue. One leader expressed his thoughts as follows:

> Too many principals think that just saying yes is support. [Program leaders] need to get them beyond that . . . . Principals need to be in the classroom. They need to say to teachers, "I saw you do this in the classroom, and the kids responded well. Tell me why you did that. What was going on?" Support has to be more that just giving them books and letting them go to seminars.

☐ Sample Expectations for District-Level Administrators

Definitive commitments for district administration might include their agreement to do the following:

- Adopt standards-based materials
- Fund materials management systems, teachers on special assignment, and substitutes
- Earmark district contract days for professional development
- Provide release time for classroom teachers   ■

☐ Sample Expectations for School-Level Administrators

Specific agreements with principals to support improvements in mathematics and science education might include the following commitments:

- Provide release time for teacher professional development
- Budget resources to support the improvement efforts
- Reduce classroom responsibilities of teacher leaders
- Allocate time and space for teachers to collaborate

- Allocate materials storage space
- Monitor classroom implementation
- Work with resistant teachers
- Educate parents about the importance of the program   ■

Engage Principals Early and Often

Principal support is pivotal in determining teacher participation in professional development, facilitating the work of teacher leaders on site, and building a supportive context for the program at the building level (Boyd et al. 2003). Leaders of mathematics and science professional development programs have sometimes learned the hard way the importance of a comprehensive plan for engaging principals. The sense of urgency about getting teachers on board can capture the attention of program leaders. They plunge into recruiting teachers, securing facilitators, planning agendas, and maintaining and improving these structures. In the process, leaders may neglect to secure support where it is needed most: from the school principal. "We took our eyes off the principals," regrets one leader. "It was not a conscious decision, but the work was so overwhelming that we focused on the professional development of teachers." The program suffered the consequences of this oversight when principals' support waned over time.

Efforts to educate principals about the professional development program should appeal to their most pressing needs. For example, new instructional practices for teachers have the potential of influencing student performance on tests. It is important to relate professional development goals to specific school improvement goals, and to demonstrate ways in which the program supports principals' routine responsibilities, such as teacher evaluation.

It is a reality of schooling that principal support is vulnerable to pressures of conflicting priorities, budget crises, and limited time. Program leaders note that concerted efforts to garner principal support ultimately diminish resistance and thus support long-term program growth. As one leader noted, activities for principals turned around "skeptical administrators who weren't convinced that anything needed to be done," resulting in a "significant mindset change among principals."

☐ Principals' Workshops

Annual workshops for principals—ranging from several hours to several days—can brief administrators on program goals, vision, and activities. Formal structures such as "administrative councils" can provide a vehicle for principals to interact regularly with teacher leaders and other professional development providers. Some programs have successfully used published professional development courses for principals. *Lenses on Learning* is one example of a modular course that addresses issues of concern to administrators as they seek to support standards-based mathematics instruction in their schools and districts (Grant et al. 2003).

One district program in California tapped into the California Science Implementation Network (CSIN), where principals and assistant principals participated on school leadership teams and in training along with their teachers. Still other programs worked intensively with a small group of principals to cultivate their support and skills for working with their colleagues, using principals-in-residence and other programs. Some leaders took principals to national conferences, to broaden their understanding of the program vision, and brought in national experts to work with principals locally. And finally, program leaders invited principals to participate in a subset of professional development activities for teachers, to enable them to learn about new instructional materials and pedagogy.   ■

□ Principals' Toolkit

The leaders of an elementary science initiative produced a "Principals' Toolkit," with the help of a committee of former principals and current district-level administrators. Principals received a user-friendly reference to select models, observation instruments, explanations, and examples of investigative science. Science resource teachers met with principals to explain how their own expertise might be enlisted on site to promote effective science teaching. Principals became very well informed about the initiative, and they often made science lessons (instead of the more typical reading lessons) the subject of elementary teacher performance reviews.   ■

Build Networks Between and Among Levels of Administration

Administrator networks tend to increase accountability among leaders, particularly in multi-district efforts where maintaining quality control can be problematic. Through cross-district communication structures, monthly superintendent meetings, and co-directors' meetings, important issues are kept on the front burner. As implementation progresses, districts are likely to assume greater accountability roles. The leader of one multi-district program commented,

> When you're dealing with a loose federation, you have to tread lightly . . . . You don't have quality control from a viewpoint of direct responsibility, but you do have good, effective communication to stimulate that.

Many programs found that distributing leadership capacity was a practical way to keep a program moving forward in the face of administrative turnover. Strategies include:

- Keeping the school board informed
- Developing networks to disseminate broadly knowledge that might otherwise be concentrated among a few individual leaders
- Involving committed mid-level administrators and assistant principals in leadership roles in the program
- Developing special programs to bring new principals on board quickly

☐ Multi-District Networks

One K–8, multi-district science initiative formed a consortium among participating districts. Joint activities included:

> Quarterly meetings of business officials and superintendents of the districts with program staff to:
> - review roles and responsibilities
> - clarify issues
> - monitor program accomplishments and timelines.
>
> Quarterly, job-alike meetings during which:
> - superintendents addressed implementation issues and received progress reports
> - business officers discussed logistical and fiscal issues
> - principals discussed "promising practices" and received additional training on content and pedagogy

A multi-district, secondary science initiative built several networking structures for administrators, which included:

- Bimonthly meetings of program directors from each district, focused on planning, professional development scheduling, and other pertinent information

- Quarterly meetings for an administrative advisory council com-
  posed of an elementary and a middle grades principal from each
  partner district

This group planned a half-day workshop to introduce new administrators to inquiry science and issues relevant to both elementary
and middle grades science. A superintendents' breakfast was also
held to provide updates on program activities and expected outcomes.   ■

Vertical Teams Within a District

Within districts, mathematics and science education leaders should
consider creating "vertical" teams. Membership can consist of
various levels of administrators: superintendents, assistant superintendents, curriculum directors, principals, assistant principals, department chairs, and teachers. In the face of mobility among school and
district administrators, these teams provide a vehicle for sustaining
awareness and keeping newcomers apprised of improvement activities and commitments. Networks such as these clarify the chain of
command, specifying who is responsible to whom, thus enforcing
accountability.

Principal Networks

Networks for principals can provide a strong incentive for school-
level participation and commitment in professional development efforts. The added value of networks extends to new administrators,
who have a chance to gain deeper knowledge of the program vision
and activities and to discover what is working for principals
elsewhere in their system. Although networks do not guarantee administrators' engagement, they do furnish opportunities to share
knowledge, align efforts, and plan improvements that can encourage
extension and continuity of administrative support.

Plan for Administrator Turnover

High levels of turnover among administrators complicate the process
of developing stakeholder support. Changes in district leadership can
blur the message about the direction of mathematics and science education, which in turn influences implementation in the schools. Yet
turnover in district leadership is not uncommon, as one program
leader explained:

> Since the project began, there has been continual turnover in su-
> perintendents and mathematics coordinators in three of the four
> districts. . . . It takes time with every transition to work out the
> kinks and get the administrators on board.

Just as turnover at the district level disrupts progress, principal
turnover interferes with development of shared understanding and
progress at the school level. One program leader reported that by the
end of several years of the initiative, "only 45 percent of principals
had been at the school since the beginning of the project." When
there is such extensive turnover, valuable time must be rededicated
to gaining support.

Build Support Among Parents

Mathematics and science education initiatives need the support of
parents. Parent support can be garnered by making the case that the
program goals match theirs: more challenging and motivating
instruction for their children. Communicating with parents and
the school community is also a preventive measure, because
misinformation may provoke criticism from parents, particularly
when changes in science and mathematics instruction result in
temporary setbacks in student achievement. As one program leader
put it,

> When you change the game—the content and mode of instruction—
> kids that had difficulty before are finding mathematics more
> enjoyable and easier. Those who succeeded at a more algorithmic
> approach are now finding it harder. So [some] parents have kids
> who are no longer getting A's and this is a problem—an emotional
> one—[and] it may not take very many of those kinds of parents to
> raise questions for the middle-of-the-road kids.

Many education improvement programs have not paid enough attention to creating parent and community support. Leaders may be
stymied by the difficulties in engaging parents. They also may be so
caught up in preparing teachers and administrators that they inadvertently neglect parents in the school community. As the program
unfolded, a professional development leader realized that parent
involvement "was going to take a lot more time and effort than we
were able to devote to it to be successful." Even though engaging
parents may seem like a distraction from the start-up work of a
program, parent support will be essential to secure the program's
future.

□ Engaging Parents and the Broader Community

To ensure public approval, one program used a highly inclusive, community-oriented process for reviewing instructional materials. Another program intentionally worked with small groups of parents to combat the negative media coverage of particular mathematics instructional materials. Program leaders brought in an outside consultant to explain the materials, organized evening meetings with parents, offered child care to encourage attendance, and used business volunteers to help run the event.

Some leaders organized broad-based advisory groups consisting of parents, teachers, administrators, counselors, union members, and other community leaders, who helped build community awareness and support. Family Math and Science Nights have covered many bases: kicking off program activities each year, demonstrating and celebrating success, distributing informational materials, and introducing parents to mathematics and science content and materials through a variety of activities. Still other programs have engaged parents as partners by inviting them to become volunteer "associates" to assist with materials management. Program leaders may also contact the media to inform parents and others in the school community about the progress of improvement efforts.   ■

Tap into the Mathematics and Science Community

Programs that draw on scientific and mathematical expertise in the community can enrich their professional development resources. Museums, for example, provide settings for professional development activities that remove teachers from the familiar world of school and inspire them to "think outside the box." Museums also provide teachers with additional resources to use during the school year. Colleges and universities can do the same, by offering professional development around inquiry-based instruction, together with in-kind support, such as space in their facilities and staffing of materials management centers.

In addition, forming external partnerships can prove to be a reliable source of support in light of administrator turnover, fluctuating policies, and shifting political climates in the district. Regardless of their capacity to provide financial support, scientists and mathematicians from partner institutions add credibility and ultimately influence community support and policy decisions. They can be authoritative messengers, endorsing the need for teacher professional development to school boards and other constituents.

Program leaders advise thinking broadly about who may be tapped in the mathematics and science community. In addition to universities and museums, consider regional and community colleges, as well as science advocacy and educational groups.

PARTNERSHIPS TO SUSTAIN THE WORK

To secure enduring partnerships, mathematics and science education program leaders need to work continuously on developing relationships and structures for collaboration. Knowing how to unite school districts with partner institutions requires collaborative practices that bridge any cultural differences in a lasting way. As some program leaders have observed, the challenge for partnerships is to "develop organizational trust that outlasts the individuals currently involved. The partners come to feel that they are making an investment in the future" (NSF 2000).

☐Institutionalizing District–University Partnerships

When federal grant funding ended, a K–8, multi-district science initiative was able to continue through a partnership between local university and district leaders. A committee of program leaders and superintendents presented financial and personnel models to the superintendents, who unanimously elected to fund two positions. A calendar-year position was created for an associate director from the university, and a school-year position for a teacher-in-residence. Once the grant ended, the new staff assumed responsibility for planning, preparing, and delivering professional development.

In one community, collaboration with the university added credibility to the new program's education philosophy and led to alignment of the university's science-related offerings with the program vision. Together, the university and the district designed courses that reflected the goals of the initiative and, through their work with the teachers, enhanced the realization of the program vision in the classroom. ■

Pursue District Policies That Support High-Quality Mathematics and Science Instruction

District policies evolve over time, in response to federal and state mandates, school board concerns, and priorities of the chain of command (such as a new superintendent). With persistence and timely input, mathematics and science education leaders can guide their districts, encouraging them to adopt policies aligned with the program's vision of high-quality mathematics and science instruction. Rather than ignoring district policy that may not reflect the vision, a more prudent approach would be to view current policies as not necessarily the "final word." Seeking continuous improvement works well in this situation. Program leaders should constantly be on the lookout for opportunities to modify key district policies in favor of greater alignment with the program vision: working on standards documents, selection criteria for instructional materials, assessments, teacher recruitment, professional development requirements, and teacher evaluation practices.

□ Advocacy for Professional Development

In one district, teacher contracts were being renegotiated, and the program advocated mandatory professional development for teachers. Three hours of professional development per month were successfully negotiated as part of the teachers' contracts. Other programs were able to guarantee professional development for teachers new to the instructional materials—a provision that was especially important in districts with high rates of teacher turnover.

In some cases, several small districts jointly established a beginning teacher program to supply appropriate training for newly hired teachers. Faculty from the local university collaborated with program leaders, so that the district's student instructional materials became the focus of science methods courses. Most of the district's new hires received their preparation through this preservice program. This arrangement with the university gave prospective teachers the opportunity to become familiar with the program vision and student instructional materials.   ■

Connect Professional Development with School and District Priorities

In Chapter 4, we offered advice on making professional development meaningful for teachers through links to state and district priorities. Rather than appearing to compete with existing priorities, program leaders can connect professional development that supports the improvement initiative to district and school priorities. Program leaders should emphasize the centrality of professional development (both intensive and job-embedded professional development) to teacher professionalism and school improvement.

Putting Mathematics and Science on the Front Burner

Particularly when districts place higher priority on other content areas, such as literacy, leaders must demonstrate how science and mathematics are "philosophically compatible," forging connections with other subject matter leaders. To remain relevant, it is necessary to explain in concrete terms how mathematics and science goals and objectives can help students achieve in other subjects. Extending professional development to include critical thinking, oral and written communication, and similar goals can be a way of illustrating that the skills teachers learn in mathematics and science professional development can serve teachers and their students well across the curriculum.

Language arts leaders can be encouraged to purchase books that support content areas. Similarly, district mathematics and science education program leaders can educate administrators on how these efforts can contribute to equity goals. A professional development program is more likely to endure if it is consistent with and integrated into district policies and if clear links are made between what is taught and what is tested. Said one program leader, "It all has to fit together. I'm not sure I knew that when I started."

☐ Working on the Work

A superintendent's stated objective was "improving student achievement across the board." Toward this end, she adopted the "Working on the Work" model (Schlechty 2002) for providing engaging instruction to students in all content areas. Because program leaders were able to communicate parallels between components of their mathematics initiative and the superintendent's policy direction, the program was deemed "completely supportive of and aligned with Working on the Work."

In a science improvement program, the focus on sustaining the initiative was directed toward connecting science with other content areas that were assessed, namely language arts and mathematics. Program leaders emphasized the use of student notebooks to foster student writing skills, and teachers examined their science units for evidence of mathematics performance objectives.   ■

Developing Teacher Leadership Is the Key to Sustainability

Mathematics and science program leaders emphasize that the most worthwhile strategy to create lasting change at the school level is to develop teacher leadership. Often, teacher leadership has more credibility with other teachers than outside intervention and can create internal momentum for change. As one program leader commented, developing teacher leaders "allows you to build a critical mass of vision." Said another program leader, "The districts are beginning to realize that they have a treasure trove of well-trained teachers who can help them sustain the growth of the project. . . . I think this is where we're going to have some lasting effects, in these people who have really grabbed on to it and become, in the true sense, leaders." Said still another, "The [teacher] leaders in math education hold a unique position. . . . The knowledge and skills gained through their work with [the program] have given them a level of expertise not known with the district before. . . . Their continuing presence is a major force in the long-term sustainability of the [program] reforms."

☐ Teacher Leadership as a Strategy for Sustainability

An elementary science initiative provided intensive professional development and support to teacher leaders over a three-year period. Teams of three or four teachers per school were immersed in science content and instructional strategies, as well as in leadership skills. By concentrating on developing leadership within each participating school, program leaders built capacity for the district and schools to sustain the effort over the long term.

A key accomplishment of a K–8 science program was opening new pathways in the profession for teachers to excel beyond their own classroom. Leadership capacity was developed via several routes: science resource teachers, science lead teachers, professional development providers and kit trainers, coaches, study group leaders, and case study writers and facilitators. Many teachers who assumed these roles became active change agents in their school districts.

In one district, the science program created a new position of middle school science specialist. When external funding ended, the district continued to support these teacher leaders, who became involved in reviewing instructional materials and conducting professional development workshops.

For some programs, building in a teacher leadership component produced a new cadre of individuals whose expertise and perspective on teaching were of immeasurable value to their districts, their peers, and their students.   ■

The Bottom Line

Every context is different. Teachers may have particularly strong or weak backgrounds in mathematics and science, they may have varying views about what constitutes effective mathematics and science instruction, and they may approach professional development with varying degrees of enthusiasm. Professional development providers, too, will have different strengths and weaknesses, varying in their content expertise and in their experience in facilitating learning experiences for mathematics and science teachers. Districts will differ in their policy environments and in the availability of resources to support professional development. Program leaders must consider the needs and opportunities in their individual contexts as they plan initiatives that will make a difference.[8]

No one said this work was easy, but it is certainly important. This guide highlights the initial work needed to create a shared vision; some principles of the design and implementation of effective professional development; and how to develop system-wide support for ongoing improvement efforts in mathematics and science instruction. The examples shared by experienced program leaders, and the lessons they learned, will help current and future program leaders design and implement efforts to improve mathematics and science teaching and learning for all students.

Part Four: Further Readings

Bond, S. L., Boyd, S. E., & Montgomery, D. L. 1999. *Coordinating resources to support standards-based mathematics education programs.* Chapel Hill, NC: Horizon Research, Inc.

Corcoran, T. B., Shields, P. M., & Zucker, A. A. 1998. *Evaluation of NSF's stateside systemic initiatives (SSI) Program: The SSIs and professional development for teachers.* Menlo Park, CA: SRI International.

Little, J. W. 1993. Teachers' professional development in a climate of educational reform. *Educational Evaluation and Policy Analysis, 15*(2), 129–151.

---

[8] See detailed descriptions of a number of mathematics and science education efforts, and the lessons their program leaders learned about system-wide improvement, at www.horizon-research.com/LSC/news/pasley2008.php

Massell, D. 2000. *The district role in building capacity: Four strategies* (CPRE Research Briefs Series, RB-32-9/00). New Brunswick, NJ: Consortium for Policy Research in Education.

Spillane, J. P. 2002. Local theories of teacher change: The pedagogy of district policies and programs. *Teachers College Record, 104*(3), 377–420.

Spillane, J. P. 2005. *Distributed leadership*. San Francisco, CA: Jossey-Bass.

Weiss, I. R., Miller, B. A., Heck, D. J., & Cress, K. 2004. *Handbook for enhancing strategic leadership in the math and science partnerships*. Chapel Hill, NC: Horizon Research, Inc.

References

Black, P., & D., Wiliam. 1998. Inside the black box: Raising standards through classroom assessment. *Phi Delta Kappan, 80*(2), 139–144.

Bloom, G. 2007. Classroom visitations done well. *Leadership, 36*(4), 40–42, 44.

Boyd, S. E., E. R. Banilower, J. D. Pasley, & I. R. Weiss. 2003. *Progress and pitfalls: A cross-site look at local systemic change through teacher enhancement.* Chapel Hill, NC: Horizon Research, Inc.

Costa, A. L., & R. J. Garmston. 2002. *Cognitive coaching: A foundation for renaissance schools.* Norwood, MA: Christopher-Gordon Publishers.

Driscoll, M., E. Humez, J. Nikula, L. T. Goldsmith, J. Hammerman, & J. Zawojewski. 2001. *The fostering algebraic thinking toolkit: A guide for staff development.* Portsmouth, NH: Heinemann.

Elmore, R. F. 2002. *Bridging the gap between standards and achievement: The imperative for professional development in education.* Washington, DC: Albert Shanker Institute.

Garet, M. S., A. C. Porter, L. Desimone, B. F. Birman, & K. S. Yoon. 2001. What makes professional development effective? Results from a national sample of teachers. *American Educational Research Journal 38*(4), 915–945.

Grant, M. G., E. Davidson, A. S. Weinberg, B. S. Nelson, A. Sassi, & J. Bleiman (Eds.). 2003. Lenses on Learning series. Parsippany, NJ: Dale Seymour Publications.

Loucks-Horsley, S., N. Love, K. E. Stiles, S. Mundry, & P. W. Hewson. 2003. *Designing professional development for teachers of science and mathematics*, 2nd edition. Thousand Oaks, CA: Corwin Press.

McDermott, L. C. 1996. *Physics by inquiry, Volumes I and II.* New York: John Wiley.

National Council of Teachers of Mathematics. 1989. *Curriculum and evaluation standards for school mathematics.* Reston, VA: Author.

National Council of Teachers of Mathematics. 2000. *Principles and standards for school mathematics.* Reston, VA: Author.

National Research Council. 1996. *National science education standards.* Washington, DC: National Academy Press.

National Science Foundation. 2000. *The challenge and promise of K–8 science education reform.* (Foundations Monograph No. 1). Washington, DC: Author, p. 74.

National Staff Development Council. 2001. *NSDC standards for staff development.* Revised 2001. www.NSDC.org

Schifter, D., V. Bastable, & S. J. Russell. 2000. *Developing mathematical ideas.* Lebanon, IN: Pearson Learning Group.

Schlechty, P. C. 2002. *Working on the work: An action plan for teachers, principals, and superintendents.* San Francisco, CA: Jossey-Bass.

Schorr, R. Y., 2004. Helping teachers develop new conceptualizations about the teaching and learning of mathematics. *AMTE Monograph I: The work of mathematics teacher educators,* pp. 212–230.

Schorr, R. Y., & R. Lesh. 2003. A modeling approach to providing teacher development. In *Beyond constructivism: A models and modeling perspective on teaching, learning, and problem solving in mathematics education,* ed. R. Lesh and H. Doerr. Mahwah, NJ: Erlbaum, pp. 141–157.

Schorr, R. Y., L. B. Warner, M. L. Samuels, & D. L. Gearhart. 2007. Teacher development in a large urban district: The impact on students. In *Models and modeling as foundations for the future in mathematics education,* ed. R. Lesh, E. Hamilton, and J. Kaput. Mahwah, NJ: Erlbaum.

Shulman, L. S. 1986. Those who understand: Knowledge growth in teaching. *Educational Researcher, 15*(2), 4–14.

Stiggins, R. 2005. From formative assessment to assessment FOR learning. *Phi Delta Kappan, 87*(4), 324–328.

Weiss, I. R., J. D. Pasley, P. S. Smith, E. R. Banilower, & D. J. Heck. 2003. *Looking inside the classroom: A study of K–12 mathematics and science education in the United States.* Chapel Hill, NC: Horizon Research, Inc.

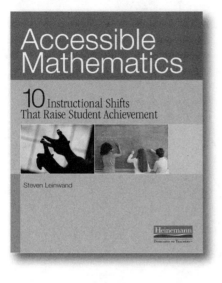